T0067812

ON THE PLAINS

MOAB

REFLECTIONS FOR THE END TIMES

Patrick Mazani, PhD

WESTBOW
PRESS®
A DIVISION OF THOMAS NELSON
& ZONDERVAN

Copyright © 2017 Patrick Mazani, PhD.

All rights reserved. No part of this book may be used or reproduced by any means, graphic, electronic, or mechanical, including photocopying, recording, taping or by any information storage retrieval system without the written permission of the author except in the case of brief quotations embodied in critical articles and reviews.

Scripture quotes marked (NKJV) are taken from the New King James Version®. Copyright © 1982 by Thomas Nelson. Used by permission. All rights reserved.

Scripture quotes marked (NRSV) New Revised Standard Version Bible, copyright © 1989 National Council of the Churches of Christ in the United States of America. Used by permission. All rights reserved.

Scripture quotations marked TNIV are taken from the *Holy Bible, Today's New International Version*®. *TNIV*® Copyright © 2001, 2005 by International Bible Society®. Used by permission of Zondervan. All rights reserved worldwide.

Scripture quotations marked KJV are from the Holy Bible, King James Version (Authorized Version). First published in 1611. Quoted from the KJV Classic Reference Bible, Copyright © 1983 by The Zondervan Corporation.

WestBow Press books may be ordered through booksellers or by contacting:

WestBow Press
A Division of Thomas Nelson & Zondervan
1663 Liberty Drive
Bloomington, IN 47403
www.westbowpress.com
1 (866) 928-1240

Because of the dynamic nature of the Internet, any web addresses or links contained in this book may have changed since publication and may no longer be valid. The views expressed in this work are solely those of the author and do not necessarily reflect the views of the publisher, and the publisher hereby disclaims any responsibility for them.

ISBN: 978-1-5127-8914-0 (sc)
ISBN: 978-1-5127-8915-7 (hc)
ISBN: 978-1-5127-8913-3 (e)

Library of Congress Control Number: 2017908346

Print information available on the last page.

WestBow Press rev. date: 07/17/2017

CONTENTS

LIST OF ABBREVIATIONS

ABD: *The Anchor Bible Dictionary*
AUSS: *Andrews University Seminary Studies*
BASOR: *Bulletin of American Schools of Oriental Research*
BC: Before Christ
BDB: *The Brown-Driver-Briggs Hebrew and English Lexicon*
c. or ca.: Latin *circa* (about, around, approximately)
cf.: Latin *confer* (compare)
CHALOT: *A Concise Hebrew and Aramaic Lexicon of the Old Testament*
COS: *The Context of Scripture*
EDNT: *Exegetical Dictionary of the New Testament*
GNC: gender-non-conforming
Ibid.: in the same source
KD: K. F. Keil and F. Delitzsch, *Biblical Commentary on the Old Testament*
KJV: King James Version
LGBTQ: lesbian, gay, bisexual, transgender, questioning or queer
NIDOTTE: *New International Dictionary of Old Testament Theology and Exegesis*
NKJV: New King James Version
NRSV: New Revised Standard Version
NT: New Testament
OT: Old Testament
TDNT: *Theological Dictionary of the New Testament*
TDOT: *Theological Dictionary of the Old Testament*
TLNT: *Theological Lexicon of the New Testament*
TLOT: *Theological Lexicon of the Old Testament*
TNIV: Today's New International Version
TWOT: *Theological Wordbook of the Old Testament*

INTRODUCTION

THE END TIMES are fascinating, and they are also scary. People constantly speculate about how things will end up. Violence escalates every moment. Natural disasters occur more frequently and with greater intensity. Human suffering is reaching unprecedented levels. The contrast between righteousness and wickedness is not only becoming more evident, but it's also increasing. In Matthew 25, Jesus speaks to only two groups on Judgment Day. Even now, we can clearly see that human beings are separating themselves into two distinct camps. People willingly decide where they will belong. Those who value righteousness are becoming more like Christ, whereas the wicked people side more blatantly with the devil.

Today, the moral decay everywhere is alarming. The battle between righteousness and wickedness, better known as the battle between good and evil, is becoming more intense than ever before. Throughout scripture, the fact is made very clear that God intervenes when wickedness reaches certain levels. When human thoughts were evil continually, God intervened (Gen. 6:5). The same is true of the depravity of Sodom and Gomorrah (Gen. 18:20). The increasing wickedness of our day cannot be much less than that of Sodom and Gomorrah on their last day. The final destruction is sure to be on the horizon.

We are all acquainted with the three divisions of time—namely, the past, the present, and the future. The Christian lives in the present, and for the future. Nobody likes to live in the past, however our history is very important to us. If we do not learn from the human mistakes of the past, we will not know how to live wisely in the present while we look forward for the coming of Christ in the future.

There is another reason for looking to the past. We need to take care that any wickedness we have done in the past is cleared up with the Lord. We must repent and seek forgiveness and cleansing from all of our unrighteous thoughts and actions (1 John 1:9). The grace of God that brings salvation exists for two reasons: first, it teaches us to shun all wickedness; second, it trains us to live righteously now while we are looking forward to the coming of our Savior (Titus 2:11). The world is in its final moments. The question then is this: "Since all these things are to be dissolved in this way, what sort of persons ought you to be in leading lives of holiness and godliness, waiting for and hastening the coming of the day of God, because of which the heavens will be set ablaze and dissolved, and the elements will melt with fire?" (2 Pet. 3:11–12 NRSV).

This book will help you to see clearly that we are living in the very last days on earth. Jesus is coming *soon*. We must learn from Israel's history and be prepared for our coming transition to be with Jesus. In particular, this book focuses on the last camp of Israel's journey from Egypt. This last camp before marching into Canaan has many things to teach us about our "camp" on the borders of the heavenly Canaan.

Israel's camp was by the Jordan River; Moses was allowed to lead them this far. In this camp, they were to finalize their preparation to cross over into the Promised Land. Many different activities, both good and evil, took place at this last camp. This book comparatively analyzes some significant events that took place at the camp on the Plains of Moab, and it shows how they relate to the drama that is going on in our world now. It also gives perspective on what we may expect to transpire in the near future as we move through the last moments of life in this old world as it currently exists. The goal of this book is to demonstrate how the historical past can help prepare us for the transition into heaven when Jesus comes.

History tends to repeat itself, but the repetitions become more intense. Wickedness and human misery are getting worse now than they have ever been. People who are preparing for the coming of Jesus tend to repeat the same mistakes made by ancient Israel when they were in their last camp. Of cause, the Bible highlights that wickedness shall increase (Matt. 24:12) and that evil people and impostors will grow worse in the last days (2 Tim. 3:13). Life is more unpredictable now. What do we do, then? We need to focus on the word of God and understand what it says about our days. We should consider biblical advice on how to live in our contemporary world, in preparation to cross over into heaven. Our aim is to be prepared to meet our Savior with joy when He comes to end the reign of sin and misery.

Spending time in the biblical lands in the Middle East makes a person understand the Bible in a new light. It is overwhelming and inspirational to stand in the very places where God had dramatically intervened in the lives of human beings. A friend, Dr. Lael Caesar, traveled with me through some of these areas, including the Plains of Moab. While we spent time in locations where biblical history was made, we discussed the events that took place there. After experiencing places where the Lord appeared, places where angels visited, places where miracles of God occurred, places where God's people lived, places where victory over enemies was granted, we could not help but give glory and honor to God.

Dr. Caesar started writing poems, expressing what he personally experienced while in the Bible lands. He invited me to also write poems. I had never crafted a poem before and did not know how to go about it. Writing poetry is not something I aspired to do, but my friend's invitation to write something about this experience was very appealing. The poem below is one of the intriguing pieces that Dr. Caesar wrote while we were on the eastern side of the Jordan River. This book is my way of fulfilling my friend's request without having to write poems.

The objective of this book is met when the reader's awareness of the coming of Jesus is sharpened, and the need to be prepared for transition to heaven is enhanced. Before we embark on a journey, we need to get prepared for it. We stand at a big advantage in that we have an opportunity to learn from ancient people's mistakes. This should give us wisdom to make wise decisions in order to avoid being trapped in similar ways.

Some important theological words and motifs are explained in this book; this allows the reader to develop an in-depth understanding of the word of God and its implications. Unless otherwise indicated, this work uses the New King James Version (NKJV) of the Bible. The end times are more complex, evil, and scary, but the Lord's grace is sufficient for us to keep focused on our faith journey. May your commitment to the Lord be strengthened, and may your anticipation for His coming be motivated. Be ready for the coming of Jesus (John 14:1–3). You can make it! I pray that you are faithful and are one of the finalists who will cross over into heaven.

I am grateful to my wife Mathrine for her love, companionship, and spiritual support. Also, I highly appreciate Hélène Thomas who read this book and made some meaningful suggestions. Above all, may God be honored!

FOR JORDAN LANDS
by Lael Caesar, PhD

Fantasy, by the camel stride, imprints,
On sand and siq, inscrutable footfalls,
Registering strokes surreal on rock-taught faces
Jilted before pubescence could provoke
Onset of features that arouse men's lust.

Reality, sketched out in farce's eye,
Defined by text of alien genius craft
Against the drop of such impregnable ground,
Need not conform to instinct, prophecy,

Logic, or final revelation. Only
Ahlan wa sahlan from Abraham to
Nabatea, Rome, Lawrence, and kingdom:

Desert, antiquity; eternity
Superimposed on fictions lived before.

Sine qua non for knowing *ne plus ultra*
Designs, upon balked trenches built to keep
Neighbors from meddling in each other's squares,
Anthropologically Rubik cubes—
Lessons in caution and humility:

Nebos for reaching heaven come in pairs,
Amorite royal bronze comes not at all,
Dhiban and Hisban hoard their fated lore,
Refine faith, science, method and tomorrow.

Over these seamless stretches minds still grope,
Joined with those mystic damned whose shaded souls
Reach out from Hor, Ajlun, Azraq, and Edom.

On Jordan's tranquil banks they stand, and long
For things they know without quite knowing how.

Chapter 1

ENEMY SPOTTED IN
THE BACKYARD

ISRAEL ARRIVED AND camped at Shittim,[1] on the Plains of Moab beyond the Jordan of Jericho (see Num. 22:1; Num. 33:48–50; Josh. 3:1). This was their final camp; the Promised Land was just across the river. The people could look across the river and see some parts of their new land. They liked what they saw. It was a long-deferred dream coming true. It was history in the making. After over four centuries of destitute immigrant life in Canaan and Egypt (Gen. 15:13; Exod. 12:40–41)[2] and four decades of wandering through the wilderness in an attempt to get

---

[1] This is the last campsite for Israel before getting into the Promised Land. The location is northeast of the Dead Sea in the Plains of Moab. This site is likely Abel-Shittim, Meadow of Acacias (Num. 33:49). Two sites have been proposed for Abel-Shittim: Tell el-Kefrein, six miles east of the Dead Sea (suggested by F. M. Abel), and Tell el-Hamman, two miles farther east of Tell el-Kefrein (a larger site proposed by Nelson Glueck). See Friedbert Ninow, "Shittim," *Eerdmans Dictionary of the Bible*, ed. David Noel Freedman (Grand Rapids: Eerdmans, 2000), 1215; Joel C. Slayton, "Shittim," *ABD*, ed. David Noel Freedman (New York: Doubleday, 1992), 5:1222–23.

[2] Exodus 12:40–41 indicates that Israel lived in Egypt for 430 years. Acts 7:6 (quoting Gen. 15:13) gives a round figure of four hundred years as Israel's time of oppression in a foreign land. However, the Jewish historian Josephus writes in *The Antiquities of the Jews*, 2.15.2: "They left in the month of Xanthicus, on the fifteenth day of the lunar month; four hundred and thirty years after our forefather Abraham came into Canaan, but two hundred and fifteen years only after Jacob removed into Egypt." In light of this, the 430 years are said to cover from the time Abraham came into Canaan to the Exodus of Israel from Egypt.

home (Num. 32:13; Josh. 5:6), they now stood at the border of the land of promise.

Despite the proximity, Israel had to remain together in their camp on the Plains of Moab for a little longer. Feelings ranged from excitement to anxiety and from tolerance to impatience. The people saw that they were so close to home, but they could not get there yet. They had to wait. They wanted to get across, settle in, and start their new lives. But the stay on the Plains of Moab was deliberate. God would make sure that they had ample time to strategize, organize themselves, and finally prepare to cross over. They had been trained now for four decades to move forward in proper order—and only when God showed that it was time to do so (Num. 2).

In that final camp, Israel had some important housekeeping issues to address. These must have been completed before crossing over. Two vital goals must have been reached while they were at the camp on the Plains of Moab. First, they received final instruction from Moses on how they would comport themselves in Canaan. Being informed of what

---

Galatians 3:17 alludes to the idea that the law (at Mt. Sinai) was given 430 years after God's covenant and promise to Abraham. It is further elaborated that:

> the time from Abraham's call to Jacob's entry into Egypt was 215 years, being the total of (1) twenty-five years lying between Abraham's call and the birth of Isaac (Gen. 12:4; Gen. 21:5), (2) sixty years lying between Isaac's birth and Jacob's birth (Gen. 25:26), and (3) the age of Jacob at the time of his migration into Egypt (Gen. 47:9). This leaves the remaining 215 years of the 430 as the actual time the Hebrews spent in Egypt. Hence the 430 years of Exodus 12:40 includes the sojourn of the patriarchs in Canaan as well as their stay in Egypt. In the time of Moses, Palestine was part of the Egyptian empire, and so it is not strange to find an author of that period including Canaan in the term *Egypt*. The translators of the Septuagint, knowing that the 430 years included the sojourn of the patriarchs in Canaan, made this point clear in their rendering of this passage: 'And the sojourning of the children of Israel, while they sojourned in the land of Egypt and the land of Canaan, was four hundred and thirty years.' An additional corroboration of the interpretation of the 430 years given above is found in the prophecy that the fourth generation of those who had entered Egypt would leave it (Gen. 15:16), and its recorded fulfillment in Exodus 6:16–20. Ellen G. White, *Patriarchs and Prophets* (Washington, DC: Review and Herald Publishing Association, 1890), 759.4.

was expected of them in Canaan helped them get ready for the new life there. Second, they needed to consecrate themselves for the transition into rest. Their survival and success in the new country was predicated on their relationship with their God. Likewise, the people living at the edge of eternity need to be informed and get ready for the transition.

Jesus spent a considerable time explaining to His disciples about the things that would take place leading to the end of time (Matt. 24; Mark 13; Luke 21; Acts 1). He also taught them, through parables, of their need for readiness at end of time. For we who live close to the end of this world's history, we must be well informed about what is expected of us. A vital and growing relationship with God is essential because it will determine our readiness for the transition to our Promised Land.

Preparing to Complete the Journey

On the Plains of Moab, Israel contemplated the journey that had started from Egypt about forty years before. Now that journey was about to be completed, people who were infants at the Exodus were now forty years old. The tedious travel from Egypt to Canaan seemed as if it had lasted forever. Many of their wilderness experiences were not very pleasant to recall. A number of significant members of their families and community had been lost due to rebellion and disobedience. They also remembered some glorious events where God mightily intervened on their behalf in dramatic ways. At the Plains of Moab camp, Israel's anticipation and enthusiasm for resettlement and rest in Canaan was high. They had the good feelings that came to finalists after a long, exhausting competition.

As the story unfolded, many who had arrived at the Plains of Moab died just before the people crossed over (Num. 25:9). They saw the Promised Land, but they could not get across; they were almost there but did not make it home. Could it be that many in our day will be so close to going to heaven but will fail to make it at the last moment?

As Israel settled into their camp on the Plains of Moab, King Balak of Moab closely observed their movements and calculated their intentions. He labeled Israel as an enemy. He put his intelligence services on high alert and kept track of every move Israel made. He was terrified by the large number of Israelites. War against them did not seem like a viable option. Numbers 22:3 says that the people of Israel were so many that Moab dreaded in fear.

Israel's intent was to simply pass by into the land across the river. God had commanded Israel that they should not harass or meddle with the people of Edom (Num. 20:14–21), Moab (Deut. 2:9), or Ammon (Deut. 2:18–19) because they were their relatives. In reality, Moab had nothing to fear from Israel at this time. So why would Moab be agitated by people who were simply passing by on their way to their own destination? What made Moab so frightened of these Hebrews? That is the question. The answer is important because it has something to say to God's people in these last days of earth's history. Think of the question this way: Why is the devil so angry against God's people, who are just passing by to the next kingdom?

Dislocated Family Ties

The people of Moab and Ammon did not welcome Israel, but we struggle to understand why. We do not know whether they still remembered or acknowledged the fact that they were related to Israel. If they cherished Lot as their founding ancestor, then we expect that they would have known about a man named Abram, who was Lot's uncle (Gen. 11:31; Gen. 13:8). The people of Israel were descendents of this Abram.

There is another reason why one would naturally think that Moab might have been happy to have Israel as neighbors. Sihon, the king of the Amorites, was a very unfriendly neighbor to Moab. Before Israel came along, Sihon had fought Moab and had taken most of their land (Num. 21:26). When Israel was traveling toward Canaan, they also met resistance from Sihon. It happened this way: Moses sent a respectful word to Sihon, asking for permission to pass through his territory on the King's Highway. Israel promised not to help themselves to his natural resources. Sihon rejected the request. Moreover, he came out with his full army to fight against Israel.

Israel's God and Israel's military were superior to those of the

Amorites, so Sihon lost the battle. The people of Moab knew about Israel's defeat of the Amorites. Their long-standing enemy was destroyed by Israel. This seemed like the perfect opportunity for the king of Moab to ally himself with Israel against their common enemy. Instead, for reasons that do not seem to bear the weight of legitimacy, Moab resisted Israel. The last part of Israel's journey to their promised land was marked by an unreasonable hatred toward them from people who might have been expected to befriend them. We have it on good authority that the same kind of unreasoning hatred will exist during the last part of our journey to the heavenly Canaan. Matthew 24:12 warns us that the love of many people will grow cold. For reasons known only to themselves, many individuals will object to genuine love and support from their families and friends. Moreover, they will be bitter against those who have done nothing to offend or hurt them.

When you help people to resolve an enigma in their lives, they may respond in one of several ways. They may express appropriate gratitude for the intervention. On the other hand, they may choose to not say anything to you about the assistance you gave. They may even assume that it is their right to have help from you. The people of Moab did not appreciate the deliverance from Sihon that Israel had provided for them. Instead, Moab's unreasonable fear motivated them to seek a way to destroy Israel.

In the last days of earth's history, people will be ungrateful (2 Tim. 3:2). You may go out of your way to help some people, but they may feel it their right to have you do so. They may not feel compelled or obligated to thank you. If they do not receive some assistance to which they feel entitled, they resort to robbing others. They do not care whether they cause harm or loss of life to those who have done nothing to hurt them. Some pay back evil for good. When the human mind is evil continually (Gen. 6:5), there is a critical loss of moral discernment. Common sense is not so common.

In ancient societies, a special group of knowledgeable, elderly folks played a very important role during times of national emergencies. Such a group was accustomed to appear before the king any time they were summoned for advice. These men were known as the "bearded," "elders," or "wise men." They usually convened their meetings near the main entrance of the gate to the city. The people could see these men sitting at the bench in the public square. The men at the bench addressed important issues and made decisions for the community. In accordance with this custom, Balak, the king of Moab, summoned his elders and counseled with them regarding the nearby camp of Israel. The elders and the king agreed to involve their neighbors, the Midianites, in their deliberations. They hoped that an alliance between Moab and Midian would strengthen their hand against the immigrant nation camped near their borders.

Referring to Israel, Moab said sarcastically, "this assembly shall lick up all that is around us as the ox licks up the grass of the field" (Num. 22:4). Later on, Balaam echoed that thought, saying that Israel had the strength of a wild ox (Num. 23:22; Num. 24:8). The Moabites expressed Israel's potential to defeat all nearby nations in a proverbial simile that any pastoral community would easily understand. When Moab likened Israel to an ox grazing in the field, they may have given some hint of a reason for their desire to eliminate the migrants. They may have worried about the possible depletion of some natural resources. Perhaps they also thought that Israel might cause economic damages in the area by looting. Moab feared that Israel would ultimately destroy everybody around them. But Israel had already passed peaceably through the area belonging to Moab and was camped on the other border of Moab. Their intent was clearly to cross over the Jordan into the territory on the other side. The question remains as to why the king of Moab made such a fuss over them.

Jim Reeves once crafted a song that said, "This world is not my home, I'm just a-passing through, my treasures are laid up somewhere beyond the blue." The question remains to this day: why is the devil so furious at God's people, who are just passing through this world?

King Balak reasoned that it was necessary to restrain Israel from getting to their destination. The enemy of God's people had his own fears. The number and unity of Israel as they came near to the end of their journey threatened Balak and his contemporaries. If God's people will remain united at the end of time, they can become a force with which to reckon. Such unity will enable them to accomplish whatever they are called to do for the glory of God. Unity is power. For God's Church, during this time of the end, unity is priority.

Unity at the End of Time

The world is entering into its final moments. Satan, the enemy of God's people, watches their lives and their motives very closely. Their number and their unity are a big issue with him. If God's people remain united, they can be an invincible force against Satan. For this reason, Satan does all he can to disrupt the unity among God's people. He also tries to capture and destroy as many as possible so that they will not be able to enter into the Promised Land. He attacks in all areas of human life and activity. Many people are familiar with the slogan: "Together we stand; divided we fall!"[3]

Dr. Ted N. C. Wilson, President of the General Conference of the Seventh-day Adventist Church, raised four concerns with the last day Church.

1. A loss of identity among some pastors and church members.
2. The growing tide of worldliness in many of our churches.
3. The danger of disunity.
4. A spiritual complacency and apathy that leads to a lack of involvement in the mission of the church.[4]

A fragmented church will suffer from punctured relationships and spiritual malaise. It will lose the battle against the enemy. God's mission cannot be advanced by a people who are not united. God's work suffers much loss at the hands of a divided Church. Disunited people easily lose their focus; they are easily distracted by activities that have nothing to do with their mission at the end times. They fight against each other

---

[3] The phrase is attributed to Aesop (c. 620–564 BC), an ancient Greek storyteller. It has since been adapted and used by many nations. In the United States of America, it was popularized by John Dickson in "The Liberty Song," a revolutionary war song that was first published in 1768 in the *Boston Gazette*.

[4] "An Urgent Prophetic Calling," Ted N. C. Wilson, accessed November 14, 2013. http://www.adventistreview.org/an-urgent-prophetic-calling.

even over minute issues. Some churches will fail to thrive and eventually close their doors for lack of members. A new believer who was joining a small church raised up her hand and read from 2 Timothy 2:23. Then she asked, "Why do you people in this church quarrel?" The leader retorted, "Someone has to stand!"

I am not an advocate of uniformity—the idea of conforming to the ways of others simply for the sake of being the same. I am talking about unity, togetherness, harmony, and oneness in spirit, doctrine, and worship based upon the principles of the Bible. The devil throws many issues upon God's end-time people to disrupt true unity. Some believers separate themselves from others because of cultural interests. Culture becomes more important to them than anything else with regard to worship. This exclusivism is common with immigrants anywhere, and even some indigenous people groups prefer to isolate themselves. Numerous believers separate themselves from other believers because of who they are and because of their circumstances.

There are some believers who separate themselves from others for worship because of their different language or culture. These same believers, however, do not isolate themselves when it comes to business, work, school, sports, or the market place. Culture becomes an issue only in the church but not in the sports stadium, industry, hospital, school, or shopping center! Jesus repeatedly pleaded with His Father that His followers "may be one" (John 17:11, 21–23). We need to endeavor to keep the unity of the Spirit (Eph. 4:3). If we can mix well in different social circles during the week, it should not be difficult to be together for worship on Sabbath. Unity calls for the demolition of overlapping regional, or duplicate, or parallel churches and administrative conferences among God's end-time church. People need to learn to not only tolerate but also love each other more and more. It is sad that some people still argue for and see mission advantages in a racially divided church structure.

God's people at the end of the world will be fragmented because of doctrinal differences, religious practices, worship styles, cultural or racial issues, and lifestyle preferences. There are many other major (or even minor) issues that will divide God's people. The Church may find itself in an ongoing struggle to keep the membership together. People who are close to their eternal home but are still waiting can become restless. Some will lose the vision they had cherished for so long. What we should know is that the enemy of God will still relentlessly seek to deter as many as he can from claiming their place in heaven, even at the last moment. Those who focus on Him in whom they believe, and on the land to which they are going, will prevail over distractions and reject divisive ambitions.

The king of Moab kept updating his intelligence as Israel settled at Shittim (Num. 22). He saw Israel as an "assembly" that covered the face of the earth (Num. 22:4–5). The king's exaggeration here is caused by fear. He saw that the options for Moab were very limited. What could he do to deter Israel from progressing into Canaan? That was the question.

Those Called by God

As Israel was coming in, the people of Moab referred to Israel as *qāhāl,* meaning "assembly," "convocation," "congregation," "community," "company," "assembled group of people,"[5] or a gathering (Num. 22:4). This is an interesting reference. The noun *qāhāl* is typically Hebrew. There has been no attestation to this word in other earlier ancient, northwest Semitic languages, including Ugaritic, Phoenician, or Old Aramaic. This Hebrew word and its derivatives were later adopted by other ancient languages. It was befitting for Israel to be referred to as the assembly or congregation. The Greek equivalent to the Hebrew *qāhāl* is *ecclesia,* which means "assembly" (secular) or "church" (biblical or ecclesiastical).[6] The concept of ecclesia comes from the Greek verb *kaleo,* meaning "call out." Ecclesia, then, is the "called-out" community of faith. The church is the called-out assembly of God's people. God called the Church to likewise call people from darkness to come into God's marvelous light (1 Pet. 2:9). The Church exists to call out people from the

---

[5] *TDOT,* 12:546; *TLOT,* 3:1118; *BDB,* 874; *CHALOT,* 314–315.
[6] *TDNT,* 3:502. In the New Testament, the Church is also viewed as the body of Christian believers. While Christians who gather together in a particular place compose a church, they are also taken as a congregation. The universal congregations belonging to the same organization compose the Church.

world (Isa. 48:20; Rev. 18:4). United, the Church will accomplish God's mission on earth. Divided, the Church will struggle to exist and to fulfill its mission. The Church must also do its best to retain and nurture those who positively respond to the call.

The Ammonites and the Moabites were forbidden to enter the assembly of the Lord, even to the tenth generation (Deut. 23:3–6). Their heinous crime was their lack of hospitality and the hiring of Balaam to curse Israel. Israel had no intentions of harassing these people because they were relatives. Later on in the history of Israel, several prophets denounced these nations at different times for their unruly behavior (Isa. 15–16; Jer. 48–49; Ezek. 25; Amos 1–2; Zeph. 2). As long as the Ammonites and the Moabites maintained their hostility against God and His people, they were not allowed to be members of the assembly of believers. Some from Ammon and Moab truly turned to the Lord, seeking to worship Him and serve Him. God would not turn these back. The story of Ruth in the Bible book bearing her name is a classic example of the grace of God that accepts anyone who makes such a commitment. Provision had already been made for the acceptance of aliens into God's fellowship (Exod. 22:21–24; Lev. 19:34; Deut. 24:17–20; Mal. 3:5). More light on the accommodation of aliens in the faith is portrayed in Exodus 20:8–11, Isaiah 56:3–8, John 1:12, and Galatians 3:28.

At the time of the end, the Church may seem fragile and fragmented. It may appear weak or ineffective. Yet it is still God's chosen institution to call people out of darkness and into God's marvelous light. Despite internal theological squabbles or external social problems, and despite persistent corruption within the Church, it is still God's Church. God's faithful people will sing songs of inspiration, preach the truth, render faithful service, and win souls for Jesus to the very end. Jesus assured us that "the gates of hell shall not prevail against it" (Matt. 16:18). At the end of time, the Church may be robbed of some of its children, and it may be harassed by Satan in every way, but it will triumph. The Church will continue its noble task of calling people from the world and making them ready to transition into a new life in Christ. The Church will successfully cross over into heaven with all who have truly committed their lives to the call of God.

Israel was comprised of twelve distinct tribes. There were numerous other people who had joined them when they left Egypt (Exod. 12:38). Still other people joined them along the way as they traveled toward the Promised Land (Num. 10:29–33; Judg. 4:11). When all of these people arrived at the final camp before entering the Promised Land, the indigenous people saw them as a unified group, an assembly. This was the outsider's perspective on Israel. God's people were an assembly despite the tribal distinctions. As long as they maintained that vital unity, the enemy of God's people would be threatened by their presence.

When outsiders see divisions and altercations within the Church, then the Church loses its effectiveness for drawing the world to Christ. While Israel prepared to cross over, enemies sought to disrupt their progress. When they camped at the border of the land they would call home, the enemy was furious and attempted to destroy them before they could cross over. Once Israel became divided and corrupted, they would be more vulnerable to the attacks of their enemies. Similarly, the Church of God at the end of time will face fierce opposition and attacks from the devil, who desires to create divisions and a lack of harmony as time is running out. Sometimes the devil brings false-hearted individuals into the Church's ranks, and these people will wreak havoc from within. An enemy inside can destroy more than the external enemy we are watching.

At the end of time, there is a growing sense of individualism, even among God's people. Easily irritated individuals choose to be independent from the main body of the Church; they sometimes confuse isolation with peace. The Church should also be aware that some of the bitterest enemies the Church will ever encounter are from within the Church itself. These enemies will come in style. Some will militate against the leadership. Fights within the Church can be very dirty and unhealthy. Internal enemies will work on offsetting the Church from its traditional biblical understanding to accommodate some social and political interests in biblical hermeneutics. Many in the Church will be more concerned with political correctness than with obedience to biblical principles. Practices which neither the Bible nor the early Church ever mentioned will surface. Many believers will try to incorporate secular practices that have not, for scriptural reasons, been permitted in the Church.

Some biblical texts will be twisted to accommodate contemporary social structures. The goal of this inside job is to steer the Church away from its Bible-based doctrines, understandings, and practices. The Bible encourages us to seek peace with everybody and holiness at all costs (Heb. 12:14). Those who seek to change the terms of biblical holiness risk separation from Jesus when He comes.

Various activities took place on the Plains of Moab while Israel was waiting for their orders to cross over into Canaan. These ranged from acts of righteousness to outright rebellion against God. A time of waiting is a time of testing. Waiting increases anticipation for some people. Waiting stirs up restlessness, anxiety, or rebellion in others. People will find something to occupy themselves while they wait. If nothing important is going on in the Church that is waiting for the soon coming Christ, then many members—even children and youth—will find themselves something else to do. Sadly, that something else is usually not good. Waiting is a good test of character, and it is also profitable for developing patience in those who are willing to be taught by it. Waiting allows us to weigh things out, reflect, refresh, refocus, rethink, and plan. Those waiting for the coming of Jesus at the end of the world are a special target of Satan. Please notice that waiting is not synonymous with doing nothing. Waiting is the time for us to be getting ready and also helping others get ready. We need to calibrate and refocus our spiritual energies. Mission must continue in earnest while we wait. We must be engaged in God's work while we are waiting for the coming of our Lord Jesus to lead us across into heaven.

Like the ancient king of Moab, Satan watches every move of God's people, all the while attempting to disrupt and destroy them before they cross over. Unfortunately, many of God's children who yield to secular life relax their relationship with God. These will fall victim to the devil just when the time of Jesus's coming is near, even at the doors. It is sad to see some spiritual giants slipping away from the faith at the very last moment of earth's history.

Chapter 2

MAGIC MAN SHOWING UP

NO SOONER HAD Israel settled at Shittim than Balak, son of Zippor,[7] the king of Moab, summoned Balaam, son of Beor, who lived at Pethor[8] near the Euphrates River in Mesopotamia (Num. 22:5; Deut. 23:4). The role of Balaam was very crucial at that time for the Moabites, as well as for the Midianites. Balaam was a fascinating person (Num. 22–24). He was a man of renown because he specialized in casting spells. Balaam had blessings and curses at his command; he was a diviner. The belief that prevailed in his day was that whatever came out of Balaam's mouth had effect, either for good or bad, on the targeted person or group. One could hire Balaam to curse one's enemies, and the curse would render them incapacitated. Balak officially invited Balaam to come to his aid just before Israel entered into Canaan.

Balak was confident that Balaam's curse on Israel would give him every advantage over his perceived enemies. Once the curse was pronounced, he believed that Israel would no longer be united. He hoped that they would be so weak and disoriented that they could be easily

---

[7] Balak, son of Zippor, king of Moab is also mentioned in Judges 11:25.

[8] A suggestion has been made that Balaam was an Ammonite based on the Hebrew *běnê-'ammô,* "sons of his people" (Num. 22:5), which is taken as a scribal error for "the Ammonites." This idea is refuted by Balaam's own words, which said that he was going back to the land of his own people (Num. 24:14). Moreover, several Assyrian inscriptions unquestionably identify Pethor with Pitru, which is located on the upper Euphrates. The biblical text supports the upper Euphrates as the home for Balaam (Num. 23:7; Deut. 23:4). Some people still think that this place was too far from the Plains of Moab, but any other alternative suggestion for Balaam's home place fails to meet the biblical criteria.

destroyed; then their plans to enter into the Promised Land would be foiled. Likewise, in the last days before the end of the world, Satan will send his envoys into the Church, to confuse, frustrate, and disorient God's people. Some of the devil's advocates will be well-respected church stalwarts who have a commanding theological tradition. These will use the Bible in subtle ways to introduce strange teachings in the Church. The idea behind this is that Satan will have all the advantage over God's people so as to mislead and destroy them before entering the promised eternal life. Even those most committed to God are not safe apart from total dependence upon Jesus (Matt. 24:24; Mark 13:22).

The Identity of Balaam

Balaam was a historical figure who was well-known at the time when Israel was about to enter Canaan. Balaam (Num. 22–24) is also cited in several Qumran scrolls.[9] Balaam must not be confused with Bela, son of Beor (Gen. 36:32–33; 1 Chron. 1:43–44). An Aramaic text on a plaster[10] was discovered at Tell Deir Alla, located in the eastern Jordan Valley. This plaster text, which is dated to the ninth century BC, mentions a prophet, Balaam, who also appears in the biblical text. This writing indicates that Balaam was a seer of the gods and that gods came to him at night (cf. Num. 22:20). The discovered plaster text on Balaam shows that his tradition was maintained for a long time in the area. Balaam had built a name for himself. He was an outstanding international figure who charmed his audiences with his intriguing performances. He was popular and consulted far and wide. He took a fee from anyone who came for consultancy (Num. 22:7). This was a widespread practice in the ancient Near East. Those who sought for the services of a diviner would always take with them a fee (cf. 1 Sam. 9:6–10). Balaam could

---

[9] Martin Abegg, Jr., Peter Flint, and Eugene Ulrich, *The Dead Sea Scrolls Bible* (New York: HarperCollins Publishers, 1999), 108–144; James VanderKam and Peter Flint, *The Meaning of the Dead Sea Scrolls* (New York: HarperCollins Publishers, 2002), 411.

[10] P. Kyle McCarter Jr., "The Balaam Texts from Deir 'Alla: The First Combination," *BASOR* 237 (1980): 49–60.

charge whatever he wanted for his divining fees (Num. 22:18). The text seems to indicate that Balaam was not inclined to make money a big issue with regard to his services.

Tell Deir Alla Text

The text reads: (1) [... The sa]ying[s of Bala]am, [son of Be] or, the man who was a seer of the gods. Lo! Gods came to him in the night [and spoke to] him (2) according to these w[ord]s. Then they said to [Bala]am, son of Beor, thus: "Let someone make a [] hearafter, so that [what] you have hea[rd may be se]en!" (3) And Balaam rose in the morning [] right hand [] and could not [eat] and wept (4) aloud. Then his people came in to him [and said] to Balaam, son of Beor, "Do you fast? [] Do you weep?" And he (5) said to them, "Si[t do]wn! I shall inform you what the Shad[dayin have done]. Now come, see the deeds of the g[o]ds!. The g[o]ds have gathered (6) and the <u>Shaddayin</u> have taken their places in the assembly and said to Sh[, thus:] 'Sew the skies shut with your thick cloud! There let there be darkness and no (7) perpetual shining and n[o] radiance! For you will put a sea[l upon the thick] cloud of darkness and you will not remove it forever! For the swift has (8) reproached the eagle, the voice of vultures resounds. The st[ork has] the young of the NHS-bird and ripped up the chicks of the heron. The swallow has belittled (9) the dove, and the sparrow [] and [] the staff. Instead of ewes the stick is driven along. Hares have eaten (10) []. Freemen [] have drunk wine, and hyenas have listened to instruction. The whelps of the (11) f[ox] laughs at wise men, and the poor woman has mixed myrrh, and the priestess (12) [] to the one who wears a girdle of threads. The esteemed esteems and the esteemer is es[teemed.] and everyone has seen those things that decree offspring and young. (15) [] to the leopard. The piglet has chased the young (16) [of] those who are girded and the eye ...'"

Balaam was a non-Israelite. He was an outsider, hired by another outsider to come and confuse God's people, who were on the verge of entering their promised land. Balak's problem, then, lies in the fact that this same Balaam is not satisfied to communicate only with Balak. Balaam also communicates with the God of Israel. He takes his cues from God's messages. He even refers to the God of Israel as "the LORD my God" (Num. 22:18). Despite Balaam's claim to kinship with God, he is nowhere in scripture entitled "the prophet" or "the servant of the LORD." The idea that Balaam might be a non-Israelite who served the God of Israel can be laid to rest here. He was not a faithful servant of the Most High God.

It is true that the God of Israel is not limited to blessing and communicating with people who are of the seed of Israel alone. In the earlier days, God spoke in a dream to Abimelech, king of Gerar, who had taken Abraham's wife, Sarah, into his harem (Gen. 20:3–7). Abraham met the mysterious king of Salem, Melchizedek, who was a priest of God Most High (Gen. 14:18–22). Abraham went so far as to give Melchizedek the tithe. God can choose to use anyone from any nation to be His servant. God communicated with Pharaoh in a dream (Gen. 41:28). Nebuchadnezzar, a heathen king, was hand-picked to be God's servant to discipline the disobedient Israelites (Jer. 25:9; Jer. 27:6; Jer. 43:10). God communicated with Nebuchadnezzar in dreams and gave him the longest outline of prophetic history (Dan. 2). God had labeled Cyrus king of Persia "my shepherd" (Isa. 44:28) and "my anointed" (Isa. 45:1) long before Cyrus ever existed.

The biblical text shows the God of the heavens interacting with people who were outside the framework of His chosen people, Israel. So it will be with the people who live in the last days. There are some people outside the confines of our religious circles with whom God is working. It is very important to remember the words of Jesus when addressing the issue of those who do not belong to our group (Mark 9:38–40; Luke 9:49–50). Moreover, Jesus said that He had other sheep outside the boundaries of His followers. The key issue is that Jesus would bring these into the fold to be one with His own (John 10:16).

There are people who are outside our church ranks who will listen to the call and respond positively. The important consideration is that those who are outside God's Church, with whom God is working, must not militate against God's will or establishment. If they are honest in heart, they will listen to God and submit to His will and leading. They will finally be united with God's true Church. God's people will hear His voice (John 10:4, 16) and respond accordingly.

The identity of Balaam, a diviner, regarding Israel is an intriguing phenomenon. He is the only man I know of who could hit a donkey until it talked (Num. 22:22–30). However, he did not prove to be wiser than his donkey. His donkey could see what he could not see. Despite his rudeness, the donkey was interested in his welfare. The Bible shows some incidents where animals are perceived to be better behaved than human beings. For example, see Job 12:7–10, Isaiah 1:3, and Jeremiah 8:7. Human beings have a power of intellect that animals do not have. To behave like an animal degrades humans to shameless creatures. God gave us authority over animals. We have the intellect and conscience. We also have moral standards from which to operate. When humans lower themselves to acting like animals, it is a sign that the world is about to end. When we fall back into the same sins again, we act like a dog that turns around and eats its vomit (Prov. 26:11). We are compared to a cleaned-up pig that soon wallows back into the mud (2 Pet. 2:22).

When Moses set out to liberate God's people from Egypt, he encountered Pharaoh's diviners (Exod. 7:11–12). We know that Jannes and Jambres (2 Tim. 3:8) showed up to resist Moses's effort to lead Israel out of captivity. These men did what Moses "did in like manner with their enchantments" (Exod. 7:11). Their intention was to frustrate and prevent Moses's plan to free God's people. Forty years later, at the end of Moses's career, Israel drew near to their destination. Once again a diviner showed up. This diviner was Balaam, and he was hired on contract to disrupt Israel's progress toward Canaan. History is known to repeat itself sometimes. In the beginning, Satan appeared on the scene and deceived Adam and Eve (Gen. 3). Satan will appear again at the close of this world's history with his subtle deceptions to deter as many of God's people as possible from pressing on toward God's kingdom. The New Testament anticipates the coming of the antichrist just before the end of the world (1 John 2:18, 22; 1 John 4:3; 2 John 7). At the end of the millennium (Rev. 20:7–17), Satan will make one last attempt to deceive all the people of the world, but he will be cast into the lake of fire.[11]

We do well to observe closely Balaam's involvement at this critical juncture for Israel. His role seems confusing. Balaam's character sometimes seems to be in line with God's prophets. He stated that he could only speak what God put in his mouth (Deut. 18:18; Num. 22:38; Num. 23:5, 12, 16; Num. 22:8, 18–20, 35, 38; Num. 23:3, 15, 17, 26; Num. 24:13). But when the men who were sent by Balak first delivered their invitation for Balaam to come with them, Balaam was not sure. He wanted to check with the Lord (Num. 22:8) to find out whether he could be of any help to Balak. The scripture records that God came to Balaam that night and asked him who his visitors were (Num. 22:9). God instructed Balaam that he was not to go with the men who had come to summon him. God gave Balaam the reasons why he was not supposed to go back with Balak's men. Israel could not be cursed because they had already been blessed (Num. 22:12). Moses informed Israel that their God did not permit Balaam to curse them but instead turned the curse into a blessing (Num. 24:10; Deut. 23:5; Neh. 13:2).

God is faithful and would not allow anyone to mess with Israel. He still maintained His promise to Abram when He called him to go to Canaan. "I will bless those who bless you, and I will curse him who curses you; and in you all the families of the earth shall be blessed" (Gen. 12:3). When God called Abram to Canaan, He promised him blessings. Now that He is calling Abram's descendents back to Canaan, God is bound by His promise to safeguard them from curses. God will place restraining orders on the enemy who wants to destroy His children. The enemy can only do as much as allowed by God. Remember the story of Job (Job 1:12; Job 2:6).

The Practice of Divination

The biblical text takes Balaam to be a "diviner" (Num. 22:7; Josh. 13:22) and a "counselor" (Num. 24:14; Num. 31:16; 2 Pet. 2:15; Rev. 2:14). He

---

[11] See Ellen G. White, *Early Writings* (Washington, DC: Review and Herald Publishing Association, 1945), 292–293.

had made a name for himself through this career. We wonder why Balaam, a diviner, wished he could have had a sword to kill the donkey (Num. 22:29). We wonder why he could not detect the sword in the angel's hand—the sword that was ready to kill him. Not until the Lord opened his eyes was he enabled to see it (Num. 22:31, 34).

Divination is the practice of successful guessing or intuitive perception. The practice of divination in the ancient times was quite complex. Divination was part of the magical arts of the time. In fact, Deuteronomy 18:10–11 gives a more complete picture of the terminology that was used for magical performances. It reads, "In you shall not be found one (who) passes his son or his daughter through fire, one practicing divination, a soothsayer, a fortune-teller or a spell-caster, or a magic charmer, or one consulting spirits, or a wizard or one inquiring of the dead." Divination was widely practiced by pagan nations including the Canaanites (Deut. 18:9–10, 14), Philistines (1 Sam. 6:2; Isa. 2:6), Babylonians (Isa. 44:25; Isa. 47:13), Ammonites (Ezek. 21:28–29), Moabites and Midianites (Num. 22:7), and other surrounding nations in general (Jer. 27:9).[12]

Divination in all of its forms was forbidden among the people of Israel (Deut. 18:10–12; 2 Kings 17:17; Ezek. 12:24; Ezek. 13:6, 7, 13). God warned His people against it. Toward the end of his life journey, King Saul, who had been rejected by God and could not communicate with God, desperately sought out a diviner (1 Sam. 28:6–10). This choice resulted in his death. The only form of divination tolerated among the Israelites was that which was specifically directed by their God. Some of the forms of divination allowed in communicating with God included the use of Urim and Thummim by the priests (Exod. 28:30; Lev. 8:8; Num. 27:21; Deut. 33:8). These objects provided a yes or no answer to the inquirer (Ezra 2:63; Neh. 7:65). Casting lots was another legitimate way of seeking divine guidance (Lev. 16:8—9; Num. 26:55–56; Acts 1:26). The process of casting lots is never explained in the biblical text, but probably this involved an object that was thrown to fall in a certain way that could determine the desired outcome.

The issue about Joseph in Egypt raises complex problems in biblical

---

[12] *TDOT*, 13:77.

interpretation. Joseph instructed his steward to look for the cup he used for practicing divination (Gen. 44:5). Joseph also intimidated his brothers by telling them that he could practice divination (Gen. 44:15). We really do not know much about Egyptian divination at the time. One popular form of divination attested by old Babylonian omen texts was lecanomancy.[13] This lecanomancy involved dropping some oil on the water in a cup to see what shapes the oil would make. An interpretation was drawn from the shapes. The Bible does not speak well of divination. In 1 Samuel 15:23, King Saul's rebellion was as serious a sin as divination.

Securing the Divine Will

Communication with the deity was crucial in ancient times. It has been crucial through all of human history. It is still crucial for us who live in the end times. God has communicated His divine will to humans through diverse methods, including His own voice (Gen. 3:8–9; Matt. 3:17; Matt. 17:5; Mark 1:11; Luke 3:22; 2 Pet. 1:17), angels (Gen. 19:1–3; Num. 22:32–35), and dreams (Gen. 28:12–13). He has also spoken to the world through Jesus (Heb. 1:1–2). God established the office of the prophet to be His mouthpiece. Moses was the prototype prophet established by God to let the people know of His divine will. Succession in this office is God's prerogative. "The LORD your God will raise up for you a Prophet like me from your midst" (Deut. 18:15, 18). The role of the prophet was not only to promote God's will, but also to monitor Israel's behavior, helping them to stay in line with the covenant law of God.

The prophet is the spokesperson for God. He or she speaks God's word; nothing more, nothing less. God will put His words in the mouth of the prophet (Deut. 18:18). God reveals His secrets to the prophets (Amos 3:7). It is clear that God monitors whatever is to be communicated to God's people. Balaam's curse words were blocked by God. Balaam was informed that he could not curse Israel because God had spoken a blessing on Israel. It is only God, or anyone in line with God, who can

---

[13] *COS*, 1:421, 423; John H. Walton, Victor H. Matthews, and Mark W. Chavalas, *The IVP Bible Background Commentary: Old Testament* (Downers Grove, IL: IVP Academic, 2000), 74.

bless or withdraw a blessing. It is only God who can make someone vulnerable to the attacks of the enemy (Job 2:6). The Bible presents tension between different types of prophets, all of who claim to be speaking for God. Jeremiah was a sharp critic against anyone who claimed to speak for God while he or she was not commissioned to do so (Jer. 23:16–18). It has not been an easy task to discern between those who claim to be sent by God and those who are actually commissioned by the King of heaven. There are several ways that can be used to detect whether or not a person is God's spokesperson. God does communicate with people; this communication serves to reveal God's will.

> There are three ways in which the Lord reveals His will to us, to guide us, and to fit us to guide others. How may we know His voice from that of a stranger? How shall we distinguish it from the voice of a false shepherd? God reveals His will to us in His word, the Holy Scriptures. His voice is also revealed in His providential workings; and it will be recognized if we do not separate our souls from Him by walking in our own ways, doing according to our own wills, and following the promptings of an unsanctified heart, until the senses have become so confused that eternal things are not discerned, and the voice of Satan is so disguised that it is accepted as the voice of God. Another way in which God's voice is heard is through the appeals of His Holy Spirit, making impressions upon the heart, which will be brought out in the character.[14]

The above passage clarifies why God communicates with people. He does so to reveal His will to us, guide us, and make us fit to guide others. In the last days, many self-styled prophets will declare themselves to be mouthpieces for God. Jesus warned the believers to be careful of such (Matt. 24:11, 24). Performing miraculous signs is not necessarily an evidence of being God's prophet. As noted above, the Egyptian

---

[14] Ellen G. White, *Testimonies for the Church* (Mountain View, CA: Pacific Press Publishing Association, 1948), 5:512.

magicians did some of the miracles Moses did (Exod. 7:10–12). During the time of the end false prophets and false teachers will be disseminating destructive heresies to deceive people (2 Pet. 2:1; 1 Tim. 4:1–2; Rev. 16:13–14). Balaam attempted to speak contrary to what God wanted him to say, but he was not allowed to do so. A safe way to detect whether a prophet is truly commissioned by God is to learn whether that prophet's words are consistent with the word of God (Isa. 8:20). Balaam was motivated by greed for profit (Jude 11). When God prevented him from gaining money by cursing Israel, he found another way to obtain a curse on Israel. He introduced false doctrines and temptations to bring evil into the camp of Israel, thus enticing them to work out their own downfall. He was successful in getting Israel to eat food offered to idols, and also in tempting them to commit sexual immorality (Rev. 2:14).

The Counsel of Balaam

Balaam was hired by King Balak specifically to curse Israel, so that Israel could be destroyed. Once Israel was incapacitated, then their mission to get into the land of promise would be aborted. Balaam never connected himself with Israel directly. He saw them from afar. He knew who they were. He communicated repeatedly with Israel's God. Before he dealt with Israel, he would first check it out with the God of Israel. This did not make him a servant of the Most High God; it simply showed that he did not want to take any chances with regard to his own safety. Balaam remained in the camp of Israel's enemies.

After setting up sacrifices on King Balak's altars, Balaam isolated himself to talk to the God of Israel. He was told exactly what to say (Num. 23:3–6). When he came back to the king of Moab, Balaam officially delivered, in the hearing of all the enemies of Israel, a speech that was nothing but a blessing to Israel (Num. 23:7–10). This happened more than once (Num. 23:18–24; Num. 24:3–9, 15–24). Before Balak gave up in anger and threw him out, Balaam uttered one of the most beautiful and long-range prophecies concerning the Messiah in Israel. He proclaimed: "I see Him, but not now; I behold Him, but not near; a Star shall come out of Jacob; a Scepter shall rise out of Israel, and batter the brow of Moab, and destroy all the sons of tumult" (Num. 24:17). Balaam was enabled to see the Messiah who would come in the distant future. Unfortunately, Balaam did not choose to develop faith in the Deliverer whom he had seen. He saw Him coming but did not believe. Many people in our day will know about the coming of Christ, but believing in Him is another thing for them; see 2 Peter 3:1–5.

Here we must stop and ask an important question: Did Balaam ever say something against Israel? We know that Balak was infuriated by Balaam's failure to meet his expectations. He dismissed Balaam with strong rebukes because he could not deliver the desired curses against Israel. Balak chased Balaam away to his own country (Num. 24:11). But before Balaam left, he gave Balak something to think about: "I am going to my people. Come I will advise you what this people will do to your people in the latter days" (Num. 24:14). What follows here is a series of Balaam's oracles which had no substance to harm Israel in any way (Num. 24:15–24). So Balaam left for his country. Later, when Israel waged a war of revenge against the Midianites, Balaam the diviner was reported as one of the casualties: he was killed with a sword (Num. 31:8; Josh. 13:22). After the death of Balaam, the army of Israel took "the women of Midian captive, with their little ones" (Num. 31:9). When the army returned from this war to their camp, Moses was enraged. He wanted to know why the soldiers had brought the Midianite women to the camp of Israel. Moses continued: "Look, these *women* caused the children of Israel, through the counsel of Balaam, to trespass against the LORD in the incident of Peor, and there was a plague among the congregation of the LORD" (Num. 31:16).

It was clear to Balaam that God protected Israel when Balak desired him to curse them. The only way it was possible for Israel to be under a curse was through Israel's choice to disobey their God. If Israel broke the laws of their own God, then they would work out their own destruction. In other words, because Israel could not be cursed by anyone outside Israel, it was only Israel who could effect a curse upon themselves. For Israel, cursing had to be an inside job. We see this motif throughout the Bible; the believer is responsible for his or her own downfall. For instance, in the Babylonian court, some officials tried in every possible way to detect some fault in Daniel's work for the king (Dan. 6:4). They failed to find anything against Daniel, yet they did not give up. They finally resolved that it was fruitless to find something that did not exist in Daniel. These men are heard saying: "Indeed we shall not find any ground for complaint against this Daniel unless we find (it) against him concerning the law of his God" (Dan. 6:5). So Daniel's accusers counseled that for Daniel to be at fault, they must craft some strategy having to do with the law of his own God. They created a law of the land that would require Daniel to break the law of his own God. Those who are waiting for the coming of Jesus will be brought to just such a test. If any are lost, it will be their own doing. They will break the law of their God in order to avoid human penalties. But those who remain faithful to their God as Daniel did will find that Daniel's God will be a shield and protector for them, just as He was for Daniel.

Balaam had to admit his utter failure to curse Israel. His final effort to save his reputation was to give some counsel to Balak, king of Moab. Counsel is shared opinion that is intended to assist in handling a situation. Counsel or advice can be either positive and effective or negative, defective, and ineffective. The person who accepts the advice is responsible for the outcomes. The client is supposed to use his or her discernment in working with the information he or she has been given. Although the blame may go to the counselor for the wrong advice, the person who executes what was suggested is fully accountable for his or her own actions. One cannot be exempted from the consequence of ill-advised behavior.

Blessing Israel

The belief that Israel is a blessed nation is revived with a new twist in our contemporary situation. To Abraham, God specified, "I will bless those who bless you, and I will curse him who curses you and in you all the families of the earth shall be blessed" (Gen. 12:3). God warned Balaam not to curse the people of Israel because they were blessed (Num. 22:12). Many believe that the nation of Israel is to have a comeback at the time of the end. This theory assumes that we will see this nation rising up in supremacy to be the head of all nations again.

Many are campaigning for the people of Israel who are settled in other countries to come back to Israel and settle there. Funds are raised to sponsor these people to relocate back to Israel. It is believed that if one gives toward the people of Israel, one will be blessed. Millions of people are being robbed of their fortunes because they hope to be blessed of God if they bless Israel by giving their funds. This false hope leads people to pray for Israel and give generously so as to receive some special blessing from God. In truth, we do not give in order to get blessings from God. We give because we recognize that God loves the needy and the unfortunate. Helping them is the right thing to do. We need to be generous to all people who are in need despite their creed or nationality. Human suffering is successfully alleviated by sacrificial love. Certainly, love gives.

Last-Day Deception

Believers have been given ample warning regarding false teachers and false prophets (Matt. 7:15; Matt. 24:11, 24; Mark 13:22; Luke 6:26; Rev. 16:13; Rev. 19:20). In the early Church, there were some controversial itinerants who were interested in advancing a different agenda from what the Church was given by Christ and the apostles (Acts 15:24; 2 Cor. 11:13, 26; Gal 1:7–9; Gal. 5:10; Titus 1:10–14; 2 Pet. 2:1; 1 John 4:1). It is clear from Christ's own words that the one who is not with Him is against Him (Matt. 12:30). This brings us to the concept of the antichrist, which simply means "against Christ" or "instead of Christ" (1 John 2:18, 22; 1 John 4:3; 2 John 7). The antichrist is an individual who is notoriously opposed to Jesus Christ and His mission on earth. In fact, there are many such individuals, and they come in different styles in the Church. The false Christ aims to deceive even the very elect (Matt. 24:24). The lawless one specializes in deceiving God's people at the end of time (2 Thess. 2:3–10). Satan is antichrist; he deceives and persecutes God's people. He works with individuals inside and outside the body of believers to destroy people who are getting ready for heaven.

The book of Revelation unveils the cosmic battle between Christ and His enemies. Satan is identified as the devil and the one who deceives the whole world (Rev. 12:9; Rev. 20:10). We have noted earlier on that Balaam appeared at the end of Israel's journey to curse them and deter them from getting into the Promised Land. Satan knows that he has a short time (Rev. 12:12). With added fury, he will appear at the time of the end to ravage and destroy the faith of God's people. It is a great consolation to know that anyone who, by the grace of God, endures the temptations and trials from Satan will be saved.

At Paphos, the early church missionaries met Bar-Jesus, aka Elymas, the sorcerer. This Bar-Jesus, who was a false prophet, opposed Barnabas and Saul to their faces. He attempted to prevent an interested officer whose name was Sergius Paulus from believing what the apostles said to him. Saul, aka Paul, rebuked the man sharply and told him that he was a son of the devil and an enemy of righteousness (Acts 13:6–12). Bar-Jesus became blind and was unable to see the sun for a while. This incident helped Sergius Paulus to believe in Jesus. Similarly, Satan, the enemy of all righteousness, specializes in blocking God's children from faith in God. This Satan will be unable to see the sun for a time while God's children are delivered into heaven (Rev. 20:1–3). The devil will be loosed from his prison after a thousand years, only to continue what he does best: deceiving people. Then he will finally be destroyed along with all who collaborated with him in opposing Jesus.

The story of Balaam is a sad one. He was a man who communicated well with God and, for a time, took his cues from God. He had a grand opportunity to commit his life to the God of Israel, but he did not do so. He never associated himself with God's people to learn more about the God with whom he communicated. Balaam was a "curser-turned-blesser"[15] (Deut. 23:5) but he chose not to trust the God who revealed Himself in such an intimate way to this diviner from Pethor. When he had utterly failed to lay a curse on all God's people who were ready for Canaan, Balaam went back to his country. He was never mentioned again except on the day when he was slain (Josh. 13:22). In the same way, Satan was very close to God in the beginning. He chose not to trust God and rebelled against Him. He will finally be seen as he really is when he meets his doom in the lake of fire (Rev. 20:10).

---

[15] Jo Ann Hackett, "Balaam," *ABD* (1992), 1:571.

Today, divination is practiced in many different forms all over the world. It is a booming business. Millions are obsessed with the idea of wanting to know how things will turn out in the immediate or long-term future. Scientific assessments, political calculations, social expectations, weather forecasts, astrological projections, economic fluctuations, business trends, and the end of the world stimulate the desire to want to know what the future holds. In social circles, occult practices and periodic horoscopes have drained from many people the desire to be independent decision makers of their own lives. Spirit mediums, mystics, or psychic powers claim to have a lot of answers. Although sought by thousands of people, these magical practices have failed to provide solutions to pertinent life issues. As time runs out, the desperation for wanting to know their fate is driving many to consult the dead through spirit mediums; see 1 Samuel 28:3–25. This has led many people into mysterious dealings with evil spirits. Demonic activities haunt and traumatize many lives everywhere. Demons intensify their activities as time runs out.

Our days are dark and scary. Despite this, our only safety is in committing our lives fully to Jesus Christ as our Lord and Savior. The Holy Spirit is willing to be with us to the very end. Our protection from deceptions by demons is guaranteed in the Lord (Isa. 41:10, 13; 2 Kings 6:16; Rom. 8:31). Indeed, "The angel of the LORD encamps all around those who fear Him, and delivers them" (Ps. 34:7).

Chapter 3

SCANDAL AT THE
BORDER POST

WHILE ISRAEL STAYED in the camp at Shittim, the biblical text reports that some of the people involved themselves in an embarrassing sexual scandal (Num. 25). As soon as Israel arrived in the camp, the king of Moab enticed Balaam, the diviner, to come over and curse them. This effort failed because the God of Israel would not permit such a thing to take place. No curse or spell could be cast on Israel without God's permission. Balak, the king of Moab, was disappointed by Balaam's failure. He finally chased the renowned diviner, whom he had hired, back to his homeland (Num. 24:10–11).

After leaving the scene of his disgrace, Balaam considered carefully whether he might find another way to claim the reward God had prevented him from collecting. Once he thought of a viable plan, he hurried back to Balak and offered a diabolical piece of advice to the king of Moab; see Numbers 31:16. Cursing Israel would not work for Balak. If ever Balak was going to have an advantage over Israel, something different must take place. Balaam suggested a plan that might actually succeed at bringing a curse upon the people of Israel. He suggested that Balak and his allies find a way to entice Israel into making a choice to break the law of their God. The diviner knew that this alone could bring a curse upon God's people. Balak believed that Balaam's plan had merit, and he set about to give the migrants opportunity to bring the curse upon themselves. Sadly, the ruse worked.

When Israel came to camp on the Plains of Moab, the nation enjoyed

God's protection from all of their enemies. At ease on the border of the land of promise, all things looked good and promising. At Balaam's instigation, the men of Israel "began to prostitute with the women of Moab" (Num. 25:1). These same women invited the men to participate in sacrifices to their gods. The Midianite women were also involved because Moab and Midian worked together to destroy Israel. It is not clear whether the women of Israel were also involved in the treachery; the text does not tell us. In that male-dominated society, women were not intentionally mentioned on many occasions. Women could be easily prosecuted, whereas men were sometimes simply exonerated after the same sexual offense. However, the laws of sexual morality prohibited both men and women from committing adultery (Exod. 20:14; Deut. 21:13–30). The offenders were liable to be punished (Lev. 20:10; Deut. 22:22–27).

Sexual Misconduct

In Numbers 25:1 the Hebrew word *liz^{e}nôt̲*, "to prostitute," "to whore," "to commit harlotry" or "to fornicate,"[16] comes from the primary verb *zānāh*, a word that also appears in postbiblical languages including Arabic, Ethiopic, and some Aramaic dialects (Jewish Aramaic, Samaritan, Syriac, Mandean).[17] The root verb denotes having sexual relations outside of a formal marital union. In fact, *zānāh* originally referred to "unregulated, illicit sexual behavior between man and woman."[18] Such an action was forbidden in Israel (Exod. 20:14; Lev. 19:29). The word *zānāh* was used especially of women when they commit unlawful heterosexual intercourse. This *zānāh* has been used of men only twice (Exod. 34:16; Num. 25:1). The parallel word usually used for men rather than women is *nā'ap* "to commit adultery" (Lev. 20:10; Prov. 6:32).[19] As can be noted, *nā'ap* has often been used in reference to a man when he commits adultery with the wife of another (Exod. 20:14; Deut. 5:18;

---

[16] *BDB*, 275–276; *TWOT*, 1:246.
[17] *TDOT*, 4:99; *BDB*, 275.
[18] *TLOT*, 1:389.
[19] *BDB*, 610.

Job 24:15; Jer. 5:7; Jer. 7:9; Jer. 23:14; Hosea 4:2). It can be pointed out that *nā'ap* has also been used of women committing adultery (Lev. 20:10; Ezek. 16:38; Ezek. 23:45). The interchanging of words usually meant either for men only or for women only may serve to indicate that both participants equally share in the infidelity despite the extenuating circumstances surrounding them. Harlotry is violently condemned in the biblical text.

Proverbs 23:27 calls a harlot *nokhrîyāh*—"an alien," "a foreigner," or "an outsider." In light of this, the men of Israel in Numbers 25:1 were dealing with women who were foreign to their marriage contract and also foreign to God's covenant community. Therefore the men of Israel who had sexual relations with Moabite and Midianite women expelled themselves from the covenant community. This had disastrous consequences. The unmarried person was never justified to have sexual relations. The married man and the married woman were forbidden to have sex with anyone else except their marriage partners. The biblical text still maintains this teaching today (1 Cor. 6:9; 2 Cor. 6:14; Heb. 13:4; Rev. 22:15). For the single person, abstinence from all sexual activities is the only way. For the married person, confining sexual activities to one's spouse is the rule. There is no exemption for anyone: sex is only for the married. If any unmarried person or a widow cannot exercise self-control over the sexual desire, let each one be legally married (1 Cor. 7:8–9).

Even though there is a clear distinction between the verbs *zānāh* (for women) and *nā'ap* (for men), they share a similar literal meaning; the action is vigorously condemned. These two words are also used similarly in a figurative sense. When Israel as a nation had improper relations with other nations, this was spoken of as committing adultery (Isa. 23:17; Ezek. 23:30; Nah. 3:4). If Israel engaged in any unethical commercial activities with another nation, whatever profit they made was taken as the hire of a harlot (Mic. 1:7). The worship of other gods besides Israel's God was taken as committing adultery (Exod. 20:3–6; Exod. 34:15–16; Deut. 31:16; Ezek. 6:9; Hosea 9:1). Faithlessness toward their God was viewed as adultery. The metaphor of husband and wife was repeatedly used to depict the relationship between God and his people. The prophets of the Old Testament were monitors of the husband

and wife relationship between God and Israel. A good example is the prophet Hosea, who belabored the message that God and Israel were related to each other just as was a husband and his wife. Faithfulness to the covenant love was top priority.

The Case for Cozbi

One of the descendants of the tribe of Simeon, Zimri, the son of Salu, congratulated himself for bringing into the camp of Israel a Midianite woman (Num. 25:6, 14–15). He shamelessly displayed himself and the woman before his tribesmen in the presence of Moses and the congregation of Israel. The name of the woman was Cozbi. Her father, Zur, was one of the leaders among the people of Midian. Zimri lured her to the camp at Shittim. It is most probable that Zimri came a bit late when he arrived at the camp. God had already started punishing the culprits for their involvement with the women of Moab and Midian when Zimri and his girlfriend showed up. There was already a crisis in the camp. People were already dying by the thousands when Zimri paraded his sin before the elders. Many of the people ran to the tabernacle, crying and in deep humiliation and contrition. They confessed their sins before the Lord and pleaded with their God to stop the scourge. Unfortunately, Zimri did not read the situation well. Clear signs all around him should have warned him against his actions, but he did not take heed. He sealed his own fate, and the fate of his girlfriend, by ignoring God's warnings. Always there are signs that clearly indicate to us whether what we intend to do is ethical. Sometimes our conscience is a good indicator to us, but we should not always trust our conscience. A weak conscience may not easily condemn us for a wrong act. Many deliberately ignore the inner voice until it is no longer noticed when it tries to warn them. When we intentionally reject God's warnings that call for us to repent, we deliberately vote for our own destruction.

Zimri refused to give up. He ignored the judgment of God that had fallen on the camp. He ostentatiously led the woman to his tent in the sight of all the people who were assembled by the tabernacle. He defiantly advanced his plan to commit adultery with Cozbi. People were entreating the Lord to spare them "when this prince in Israel flaunted his sin in the sight of the congregation, as if to defy the vengeance of God and mock the judges of the nation."[20]

Zimri reached a point of no return. Nobody could convince him to quit perpetuating the sin that was so devastating. Zimri knew that what he was doing was wrong, but he would not stop. One of the disturbing signs of the last days is that many people who know God's truth will decide to live contrary to the beliefs to which they subscribe. They do not quit sinning even though they have full light that what they are doing is very wrong.

Some justify their disobedience to God's word by quoting scripture texts out of context in order to support their convictions. This may give temporary peace of mind, but God will hold us accountable to our actions, whether good or bad (Eccl. 12:14; Matt. 12:36; Acts 17:30—31).

Like Zimri, many will not give up offenses of incredible depravity despite their knowledge of God's word. The scripture puts it this way:

> For it is impossible for those who were once enlightened, and have tasted the heavenly gift, and have become partakers of the Holy Spirit, and have tasted the good word of God and the powers of the age to come, if they fall away, to renew them again to repentance, since they crucify again for themselves the Son of God, and put Him to an open shame (Heb. 6:4–6).

When we allow ourselves to have a depraved mind, it will be very difficult for us to see where we are wrong, and even more difficult to accept correction. Deep rooted spiritual problems are not easily overcome. However, the Holy Spirit will help us defeat sin if we cooperate with Him. There are three steps people usually take in driving away the Holy Spirit. First, we ignore the Holy Spirit. When the promptings of the Holy Spirit continue, we resist. Finally, we reject any suggestions from the Holy Spirit. When we go through this cycle, we may come to a position where the Holy Spirit leaves us for good. We reach the point of no return

---

[20] Ellen G. White, *Patriarchs and Prophets* (Washington, DC: Review and Herald Publishing Association, 1958), 455.

and consistently refuse to be influenced by the Holy Spirit. When we do this, we seal our own fate.

We do not know whether Cozbi understood what was going on in the camp of Israel when she arrived. We do not know anything about her religious or ethical commitments. Cozbi may have been unmarried. The text introduces her as the daughter of Zur (Num. 25:15) and nothing more. She was a daughter of a very respectable person in his own nation. Today, the misbehavior of the children of renowned people goes viral on social media. Zimri's marital status remains unknown. Even if he were single, he would not have been exempt from sexual sanctity. Oftentimes single people feel no compunction to practice self-control in their sexual relations because they do not breach any marital commitments. The Bible indicates that it is best for the single to remain so, but if one wants to marry, it is highly commendable (1 Cor. 7:7–9). The idea of an unmarried man and woman cohabiting is a biblical taboo. When wrong behaviors are taken as normal, then we should know that we are very close to the end of everything (Matt. 24:12).

Zimri and Cozbi displayed themselves like celebrities as they walked to Zimri's tent. At this time, God had already commanded that offenders were to be destroyed. Many of those who had been involved in the sex scandal were suffering from a terrible terminal disease; people died by thousands. One of Aaron's grandsons, Phinehas, the son of Eleazar, could not stand the sight. He left the congregation and in "righteous anger" followed after Zimri and Cozbi. He picked up a light spear in his hand. Upon entering the tent, Phinehas thrust the spear through Zimri and Cozbi. They both died on the spot for illicit sex. Psalm 106:28–31 recounts this incident dramatically. The record has it that twenty-four thousand died from the plague sent by God to destroy all who were involved in the sexual debacle (Num. 25:9). These could not enter the land of promise, although they came to the very border.

Later, Moses sent the armies of Israel to fight against the Midianites, who were becoming a menace to Israel before they crossed the Jordan River into the land of promise. The army had resounding success and the warriors came back to the camp at Shittim with evidence of their victory over Midianites. Moses was angry when he saw that the men had spared the Midianite women for themselves. He said, "Look, these women caused the children of Israel, through the counsel of Balaam, to trespass against the LORD in the incident of Peor, and there was a plague among the congregation of the LORD" (Num. 31:16). The soldiers felt wholly justified in bringing these women—the spoils of battle—into the camp. Moses stood firm against this practice. Many times people seek ways of legalizing or pacifying evil. However, it is always safe for us to abide within the confines of God's word. Compromising with evil is evidence of lost moral integrity. It does not matter how these women came to Israel's camp, whether they were lured by unruly men of Israel like Zimri, or they were prisoners of war. It was not appropriate in any way to commit adultery with any of these women.

End-time Sexual Scandals

The sexual scandal that took place on the Plains of Moab is characteristic of what often happens just before God's judgments are poured out, as portrayed in the biblical text. The mixed marriages between those who followed God and those who did not were offensive to God (Gen. 6:1–7). The flood wiped out all evil people. The people of Sodom and Gomorrah and surrounding cities were known for their monstrous sexual depravity (Gen. 19). There, something strange was happening. Men were cohabiting with other men (Gen. 19:5). A conflagration of fire cleaned up those cities. At a party, Belshazzar hoarded wives and concubines, drank wine from God's vessels, and worshipped idols (Dan. 5). That very night of October 13, 539 BC, the city of Babylon fell into the hands of the Medes and Persians. When addressing the issues pertaining to the end of the world and Christ's return from heaven, Jesus cited the marrying and giving in marriage that was practiced by the people of Noah's time (Matt. 24:37–39). Jesus concluded that humanity's perversion of God's plans for relationships would be equally bad toward the end of the world. Wickedness will increase as many fail to love and obey God (Matt. 24:12).

Today, millions are sexually abused and harassed daily. Sex trafficking, sex slaves, sex predators, sex revolutions, incest, and child molestation are rampant. Marital infidelity has reached outrageous proportions. So many married people are failing to keep their commitment that the divorce rate is escalating every moment. Many legally married people divorce legally, and get legally remarried, only to divorce legally again. It goes on and on, some to fourth or fifth marriages! Some women have had five husbands, and the one they cohabit with now is not their husband (John 4:18).

People are obsessed with sexy commercials on television, the Internet, billboards, cell phones, and other personal devices. Sexy movies and pornography are booming businesses and are addictive. Those who want their products to sell fast or to catch public attention usually use sexy advertisements. It seems that people think sex, talk sex, work for sex, and live for sex all the time. Many are addicted to this hideous blot. Sex scandals brood disastrous consequences. Families are destroyed. The children of the involved parents are traumatized by experiencing the ruptured relationship between their parents. Churches lose credibility. It is bad, and it's getting even worse!

The clergy who are involved in sex scandals do great damage to the Church. Surprisingly, when the same clergy who are convicted of sex offenses are disciplined, they want to be fully rehabilitated back into the ministry. They claim that they settled their issue with God. Men and women who cohabit without benefit of marriage have become the norm for the society. Sex dominates many industries, including the clothing industry, the cosmetic industry, the food industry, the music industry, TV commercials, and movies. Legal and illegal literature circulates everywhere. Even in this age, when the sexual revolution is considered normal, God's law still stands. The sexually immoral will not enter the kingdom of heaven (1 Cor. 6:9–10; Gal. 5:19–21; Rev. 22:15). Prostitutes, whether male or female, have no place in heaven. Many people in the last days have caught the Zimri Syndrome. They know that what they are doing is wrong, but they will not repent.

Many people who are involved in illicit sexual relations have no commitment for lasting relationships. Those who stay with each other illegally for a long time dull their consciences; they no longer recognize their wrong relationships. But again, God's standard is firm and does not change to accommodate rebellion's new normal. A man and a woman who marry are accepted by God when they move in together (Gen. 2:24;

1 Cor. 7:9). A boyfriend and a girlfriend should go through the legal marital process first if they want to share the same bed.

The idea of people burning with sexual attraction for people of the same gender is not clear at the Plains of Moab. If it was an issue, I am sure Moses would have mentioned it, for provision was already made to address that problem (Lev. 18:22; Lev. 20:13; Deut. 22:5). The issue of same-sex marriage has ruptured many faith communities today and divided many nations. It will worsen as time runs out. It is legalized and has come to be accepted in society as normal. Any objection to same sex marriages is considered a hate crime and is liable to a lawsuit. But the Bible is clear about God's perspective on this. The Greek word used is *arsenokoitēs*, "one who lies with a male, a sodomite."[21] Specifically, *arsenokoitēs* refers "to a male who engages in sexual activity with men or boys."[22] The issue damned here is that of same-sex marital relations. The Bible unequivocally condemns this practice (1 Cor. 6:9–10; 1 Tim. 1:10). When humans choose to live like irrational animals (Rom. 1:26–27), God will surely put an end to history soon. It will not be long.

The lesbian, gay, bisexual, transgender, questioning or queer (LGBTQ) community cries foul against the Church and the society today. Many members of this community feel bullied, condemned, discriminated, harassed, and rejected. Unfortunately, there is no biblical support for such a lifestyle. It is true that the Church is failing to treat these individuals with dignity as Jesus did. Jesus loved and embraced the blamed wrong doer. We can learn from how He treated an individual with an immoral sexual practice. Jesus loved, forgave, and said to the one who was damned for illicit sex, "Neither do I condemn you; go and sin no more" (John 8:11). Notice that Jesus did not condemn the individual but warned her to quit doing wrong. That is love, and love corrects. The way forward is crucial and should be adhered to with humility, "go and sin no more." It is a blessing to accept correction. It brings us peace. Complying with God's standard is pertinent to our own salvation. We should not be in the business of condemning and attacking each other.

---

[21] Harold K. Moulton, *The Analytical Greek Lexicon Revised* (Grand Rapids, MI: Zondervan, 1990), 53.

[22] *Exegetical Dictionary of the New Testament*, 1:158.

Rather, we should lovingly, humbly, and prayerfully assist each other to overcome any unbiblical lifestyle.

End Time Marital Commitment

Marriage will continue as long as there are people on planet earth. Marriage is a good thing and was instituted by God Himself for the purpose of procreation. There are ample guidelines for marital relationships in the Bible, and only God can define marriage. Any model of marriage that deviates from the standard in the Bible is fraudulent and counterfeit. The breach of the biblical principles regarding marriage has caused insurmountable problems for humans everywhere. Some deviant behaviors with regard to marriage have perverted our humanness. God will stand with His word. Our task is to adhere to the marriage prescription God gave us. Any marital practice differing from the biblical model falls short of the glory of God. We may like it our own way. We may legalize it. But if it does not fall within God's definition of what marriage is, then we are living a lie and falsifying the marriage covenant. Counterfeit marriages do not glorify God. Jesus Christ has designed and commanded only the marital relationship between a man and a woman to be the reflection of the relationship between Him as the bridegroom and the Church as the bride.

The marriage relationship is one of the most important human ties among all nations of the world. Distortion of the original plan of God for this institution has been deliberate. The Bible instructs us that "Marriage is honorable among all, and the bed undefiled; but fornicators and adulterers God will judge" (Heb. 13:4).

What does the Bible say about divorce? This is a billion-dollar question. Divorce is a pain and emotionally wrecks those who are involved. It devastates the children. The pain, anguish, and suffering caused by divorce is impossible to measure. The Bible does allow for divorce, but only if a partner was involved in adultery (Matt. 5:32; Matt. 19:7–9). Even then, it does not *require* divorce. God's desire is for repentance and reconciliation. Jesus is very clear that a man or woman should not divorce his or her spouse, except if the spouse had sex with another person. The painful truth is that any couple who has divorced for reasons other than marital unfaithfulness must remain celibate if they wish to retain the blessing of God, never marrying any other person. Whoever legally marries a divorced man or a divorced woman commits adultery unless that person had biblical grounds for divorce (Matt. 19:9). In fact, the Bible has no explicit teaching on remarriage after divorce. Legalizing any relationship condemned by God does not make God change His law. When human beings legalize something that God calls wrong, it will never make it right. Any marriage overriding the marital prescription in the Bible is an adulterous relationship. When the disciples understood divorce as taught by Jesus, they concluded that it was better not to marry (Matt. 19:10). It is true that

> a woman may be legally divorced from her husband by the laws of the land and yet not divorced in the sight of God and according to the higher law. There is only one sin, which is adultery, which can place the husband or wife in a position where they can be free from the marriage vow in the sight of God. Although the laws of the land may grant a divorce, yet they are husband and wife still in the Bible light, according to the laws of God.[23]

Marriage and the Sabbath are the two holy institutions from Eden (Gen. 2). These are grossly violated in the end times. Both marriage and the Sabbath are deliberately distorted and substituted by counterfeit representations. Sabbath remains a sign between God and His people. Marriage between a man and a woman is God's symbol for the relationship between God and His Church. Jesus is depicted as the bridegroom, and the Church is the bride. Those who perverted marriage at the border of Canaan could not be allowed to enter the land of promise. Likewise, those who abuse marriage will not cross over into the heavenly Canaan. Someone who sincerely prays, but remains in an adulterous relationship, should think seriously about texts like Psalm

---

[23] Ellen G. White, *Adventist Home* (Hagerstown, MD: Review and Herald Publishing Association, 1952), 344.

66:18, Proverbs 15:8, Proverbs 28:9, John 9:31, Galatians 3:10, James 2:10, and Revelation 22:14–17.

Balaam advised Balak to lure the Israelites into sexual misconduct and idol worship because he knew that these sins would bring the curse that God had not allowed him to pronounce. The wrath of God fell with full strength on Israel when they denied their faith in that way. The incident at Shittim claimed twenty-four thousand lives. It could have been worse if it was not for Phineas, who rebuked this horrific behavior by slaying Zimri and Cozbi. God gave Phineas the credit for this action that brought peace between God and Israel (Num. 25:11–15). Balaam crafted a deadly scheme against Israel because he "loved the wages of unrighteousness" (2 Pet. 2:15). It seems that Balaam's influence went viral.

Wrong food and illicit sex have exerted their baleful influence from that time to this. Caution is given to the Church at Pergamum for subscribing to Balaam's teaching: "But I have a few things against you, because you have there those who hold the doctrine of Balaam, who taught Balak to put a stumbling block before the children of Israel, to eat things sacrificed to idols, and to commit sexual immorality" (Rev. 2:14).

Chapter 4

CALL TO WORSHIP

BALAAM, THE HIRED prophet from Mesopotamia, arrived in Moab to see what he could do to help Balak, the king of Moab, get rid of his self-styled enemies. Balak went out to meet with Balaam at the border city near the Arnon River. He chided Balaam for being hesitant to come in response to his invitation (Num. 22:37). It seems that Balak had anger issues. Instead of appreciating the "magic man" for coming, Balak found fault with him for delaying.

Anger is a corrosive emotion. Those who are traumatized by anger in their lives find it difficult to appreciate others. It is impossible to be angry and grateful at the same time. Balak could not even be grateful for getting what he wanted. Many people today have this "Balak Syndrome" and exhibit paroxysms of anger over insignificant issues. They are angry and dwell constantly on the negative side of things. They always find fault with others. Critics have difficulties in being thankful. We read in the Bible that many people in the last days will be ungrateful (2 Tim. 3:2). Despite this contemptuous spirit, God is kind to the ungrateful (Luke 6:35). God extends His loving call to all, bidding them to worship Him alone.

A Prominent Canaanite God

Balak offered several oxen and sheep and gave some gifts to Balaam, and to the princes who had been instrumental in bringing Balaam with them (Num. 22:40). The next day, Balak took Balaam to the high places of Baal, where he could see the vast camp of Israel spread out over the plain. Baal is believed to have been the most popular and powerful Canaanite god of storm and fertility. His name means "lord," "master," "owner," or "husband," signifying "a state of ownership or social superiority."[24] Excavations in the vast area of the Middle East and the Mediterranean region have provided many different figurative representations of Baal. Sometimes Baal was represented by an image of a bull, or a warrior who is holding a club in his right hand and a spear on his left hand.

It is intriguing to note how popular Baal was in the ancient world. Baal was believed to be a kingmaker, protector, benefactor, and donator of offspring.[25] Baal was also perceived to have power over weather, wind, clouds, storms, lightning, dew, fertility, vegetation, rain, and snow.[26]

Worshippers of Baal centered all their lives and activities around this god. The high places of Baal were the sites where Baal was worshipped. Some of these sites were on elevated locations, or on top of mountains. It should be noted that of all the Canaanite gods mentioned in the Old Testament, Baal is the most prominent one. The prophets of God aggressively denounced this god.

Once Balak and Balaam arrived at the high place of Baal, the diviner became the commander, and the anxious king chose the role of servant. Balaam instructed Balak to build seven altars and offer a bull and a ram on each (Num. 23:1–2). When Balak had seen that these orders were carried out, Balaam left and went to a distant place, where he met and talked to the God of Israel. Balaam was well informed and knew that the God of Israel would not communicate with him where Baal was worshipped (Num. 23:3–6; Num. 15). The jealous God of Israel would not take part in anything that would cause confusion among the attendants. They needed to know that this God had no association with Baal. He had no respect for idols. Indeed, the God of Israel met Balaam and gave him a very definite message to carry back to the king of Moab (Num. 23:5–10, 16–24).

Why did Balaam keep building and sacrificing on the altars of Baal? It is not mentioned anywhere that he ever communicated with

---

[24] Mark Anthony Phelps, "Baal," *Eerdmans Dictionary of the Bible* (Grand Rapids: Eerdmans, 2000), 134.

[25] W. Herrmann, "Baal," *Dictionary of Deities and Demons in the Bible* (Leiden: Brill, 1999), 134.

[26] Ibid.

Baal. There is no record of Baal as having said anything regarding this incident. Of cause, an idol does not talk (Ps. 115:4–8). Perhaps Balaam was simply requiring that which he knew the king expected before proceeding with the real business of finding out what the God of Israel would permit him to say regarding Israel. There is no scriptural clue to provide a definitive answer.

It can be ascertained from the biblical text that Baal worship "was characterized by sacral prostitution and by eating a sacrificial meal, by means of which an intimate relationship was established between the god and his worshippers"[27] (see Num. 25). Later on, when Israel was in the camp at Shittim, the men engaged in an unprecedented immorality with the women of Moab and Midian. These same women lured the men of Israel to worship and sacrifice to their gods. Baal-peor, or Baal of Peor, was a geographical designation for the god Baal. It is clear that Baal was worshipped at Mount Peor in Moab, east of the Dead Sea (Num. 25:3, 5; Deut. 4:3; Ps. 106:28; Hosea 9:10).

What Is Worship?

Balaam was a professional religious practitioner, and he knew how to play his religious cards well. Balaam acted like a good chaplain. A chaplain is that spiritual guy who meets and supports anybody, no matter where people are religiously. Balaam had altars built and sacrifices offered to meet the king of Moab's religious expectations. King Balak worshipped Baal, a Canaanite god, and Balaam met him where he was. On the other hand, Balaam talked about the God of Israel and was eager to know and follow His cues. We see in Balaam a syncretistic religion. Balaam coalesced the worship of Baal and the God of Israel. Why God worked with this guy and did not rebuke him about double-dealing with Baal is a puzzle. Balaam, as we have seen, gave orders to set up sacrifices at Baal's worship center. He left that place to go away to communicate privately with the God of Israel. He actually managed to communicate with Israel's God. He then came back to Baal's sanctuary and continued to facilitate worship there. This sounds like many of us

---

[27] M. J. Mulder, "ba'al," TDOT (Grand Rapids: Eerdmans, 1977), 2:194.

today. We worship God, but then we take the liberty to occasionally incorporate in our lives evil from the devil.

The idea of worship intrigues human beings. We tend to worship anything that fascinates us. We still have plenty to learn from the Hebrew Bible about worship. The word for worship is *shāḥah*, which carries the idea of bowing down before, or prostrating. In a theological sense, *shāḥah* means "to be brought low in the sense of being humbled,"[28] implying "to have one's arrogance knocked out."[29] It is necessary to have the proper attitude for worship (Isa. 2:11; Prov. 29:23; Matt. 23:12; Luke 14:11). Worship is emptying oneself before God. There are several other words that are used to describe worship, including *segad*, "to prostrate" (Isa. 46:6; Isa. 44:17, 19). The Aramaic component of *segad* implies falling down (Dan. 2:46; Dan. 3:5–7, 10, 15, 18, 28). Also, *'abād ('abōda)* is the same word for either to serve or to worship (Ps. 97:7). The Greek component *proskuneo* means to "do reverence or homage by kissing the hand"[30] or the ground.[31]

Worship is at its best when we humble ourselves and bow down in complete surrender to God, acknowledging Him alone as our God and invoking praises to Him for who He is and for all He does. Worship is our extemporaneous response of awe in the presence of God, who is our ultimate and supreme authority, deserving of all glory, honor, and majesty forever.

From ancient times, the word *worship* "expressed the oriental custom of bowing down or casting oneself on the ground, as a total bodily gesture or respect before a great one (Gen. 18:2; Exod. 18:7; 2 Sam. 14:4)."[32] Further, the verb *worship*

> always refers to an action/attitude directed toward a
> human or divine figure who is recognized (appropriately
> or inappropriately) as being in a position of honor or

---

[28] *TWOT*, 2:915.

[29] Ibid.

[30] Moulton, *The Analytical Greek Lexicon Revised*, 350–351.

[31] *The International Standard Bible Encyclopaedia* (1960): 5:3110.

[32] D. G. Peterson, "Worship," *New Dictionary of Biblical Theology* (Downers Grove, IL: InterVarsity Press, 2000), 856.

authority. Depending on the figure and the situation, it may be a gesture of greeting, respect, submission, or worship. The action may entail falling to one's knees, in front of which one places the hands or between which one bows the face (nose, forehead) to the ground (or comparable gesture), as shown by the frequent reference to "the ground" (*'ereṣ*) and "nose, face" (*'appayim*; see Gen 19:1; 1 Sam 25:23, 41; cf. 1 Kgs 18:42). The gesture is an external sign of the inner spirit (though hypocrisy is possible); the word can also simply express the inner attitude. The prayer posture (hands outstretched) normally does not entail prostration.[33]

We have noted that worship was formerly used for reverence or honor done to humans as well as to God.[34] Fear and love usually prompt worship to both humans and deity. Worship is expressed in feelings and action. Basically, worship "comprises two elements, the inward feeling of the heart, and the outward expression of it in outward sign."[35] Caution must be taken when it comes to feelings. The God of heaven is most interested in the inner beauty and purity of our hearts when we worship Him. God reads our motives and desires. It is interesting to note that in Israel, worship "consists in *a dialogic interaction* in which both parties are fully present, both parties are to some extent defined by the other, and both parties are put to some extent at risk by the transaction."[36] When people worship God in spirit and in truth (John 4:24), God is there and responds. God and people are partners in worship because they are bound by the covenant relationship.

When people are spiritually and morally sound, God is not ashamed to call them His people (Heb. 2:11). When God speaks in worship, He

---

[33] *NIDOTTE*, 2:43.

[34] James Hastings, *A Dictionary of the Bible* (New York: Charles Scribner's Sons, 1903), 941.

[35] *A Concise Cyclopedia of Religious Knowledge*, ed. Elias Benjamin Sanford (Hartford: S. S. Scranton, 1916), 973.

[36] Walter Brueggemann, *Worship in Ancient Israel: An Essential Guide* (Nashville: Abingdon, 2005), 9.

discloses Himself, He declares His will, He instructs His people, He gives them His promises, He forgives their sins and iniquities, He accepts them and their offerings, He blesses them, He glorifies Himself, and He does much more for them! God's presence is overwhelming. People respond to God by confessing their sins and affirming God's sovereignty and holiness. Worship evokes verbal praise and material response to God. Believers praise God for who He is and for what He does. They present their petitions to God and behave the way God wants them to behave.

Worship is not only vocal expression; it is the life we live in honor and obedience to God. Worship is our response to God's grace and is our acknowledgement of God's mighty deeds in our favor. God's ultimate goal for our worship experience is that we will be transformed. He has designed true worship as a means of making us godly—like God in character. "Higher than the highest human thought can reach is God's ideal for His children. Godliness—godlikeness—is the goal to be reached."[37]

Worship should not be seen as an event that comes and goes. It must encompass all that we are in every moment of every day. The visible forms of corporate worship must be backed up by our appropriate behavior, which is consistent with God's will at all times and in all places. Worship involves dethroning the self and everything else and enthroning God as Sovereign and Creator. Fearing God is the essence of worship. This kind of fear is expressed in reverential attitude towards God as the supreme arbiter for human behavior. See Revelation 14:7 and Revelation 15:4.

Place for Worship

In Deuteronomy 12, Moses describes God's expectations with regard to worship after Israel gets into Canaan. First and foremost, they were to destroy all venues that were used by the Canaanites to worship idols. All of the altars and idols were to be completely destroyed (Deut. 12:2–3). There were two crucial issues that God's followers in the Promised Land had to bear in mind. First, as stated in the Ten Commandments given

---

[37] E. G. White, *Education* (Mountain View, CA: Pacific Press Publishing Association, 1903), 18.

at Mount Sinai, there was no room given to bowing to any other god except the God of Israel (Exod. 20:4–5; Exod. 34:14; Deut. 4:19; Deut. 5:9; Deut. 8:19; Deut. 11:16; Deut. 30:17). Worshipping other gods in Canaan would incur disastrous consequences for individuals involved, and even for the entire nation. Second, there would be a designated place where all Israel would worship God. To this designated place, people were to bring their tithes, sacrifices, and offerings in response to God's blessings in their lives (Deut. 12:6–12; Deut. 14:22–29; Deut. 18:1–8; Deut. 26:1–15).

The idea of choosing a place for worship is a major theological motif in Deuteronomy. Moses emphasized the importance God attached to appropriate worship in His chosen place by repeating to the people all of His counsels in this regard. It was one of the aged leader's last acts while they were yet in their last camp beyond the Jordan. Take note that it was the Lord who would choose such a place (Deut. 12:18, 26; Deut. 14:25; Deut. 15:20; Deut. 16:7, 16; Deut. 17:8, 10; Deut. 18:6; Deut. 31:11). God chooses the *place* He wants to be worshipped, and God prescribes the *way* in which He wants to be worshipped.

Earlier, during the time of Abraham, God had told Abraham to sacrifice his son Isaac on the region of Moriah (Gen. 22:2). It is interesting to note later that when David was king of Israel, around 980 BC he saw an angel standing in Araunah's field near Jerusalem. David confessed his sin. That same day, Gad the prophet came to David and told him to build an altar for God at the same spot where he saw the angel. David consented and offered to buy the land, and he built an altar there for sacrifices (2 Sam. 24:17–25). This same place is identified as Mount Moriah, where the temple was built (2 Chron. 3:1). God unequivocally chose the place where He wanted to be worshipped, as He had promised the people through Moses. Even in our day, we should not give up coming together at our local designated place of worship because the coming of Christ is approaching so fast (Heb. 10:25).

Worship Contest at the End of Time

It was very important for Moses to reiterate the importance of proper worship. Israel was at their final camp, and they had to ready themselves for the transition into the land of promise. Worship has always brought decisive moments to anyone facing some crisis. Those of us who are living at the end times and anticipating the transition into the heavenly Canaan must recognize worship as a vital component of our spiritual existence. Whom we worship and how we worship define the course of our walks of faith. We need to remember that Jesus's last temptation in the wilderness was on worship (Matt. 4:8–10). The devil wanted Jesus to worship him. Jesus reminded the devil that worship was designed for the Lord God alone. Similarly, in the last days, worship will be a crucial issue for God's people. No doubt the devil will mount a vigorous campaign to receive worship near the end of time.

Satan has blinded the minds of many in our contemporary world so that even the good news about Jesus is not easily discerned (2 Cor. 4:4). Of course, the devil "will transform himself into an angel of light" (2 Cor. 11:14). To transform himself might imply an intentional change in his apparent character or his appearance. However, his objective is to deceive even the very elect of God (see Matt. 24:24). Ranko Stefanovic points out that "the last crisis of the world which, as the end draws near, will be characterized by the intensification of demonic activities"[38] (Rev. 9:20–21). It is disturbing to note that many people are tormented by the devil and his demons, but they still continue worshipping the same evil forces. We all need a deep understanding of what worship really is. We worship God here on earth, but we are not alone in doing this. There was worship in heaven before earth was created. When we get to heaven, worship will flow from the redeemed in unison with all creatures and angels. The New Testament does not in any way depart from the Old Testament teaching with regard to the one whom we worship. It is the same God. Worship must be done correctly and reverently. There is no room for carelessness when we approach God. We need to acknowledge Him for being who He is.

Worship can take many forms, but it always implies the idea of giving allegiance to the one worshipped. "Your Worship" can be used as a term of respect for a magistrate or mayor. Sometimes it is used loosely in referring to someone who only imagines himself or herself

---

[38] Ranko Stefanovic, *Revelation of Jesus Christ: Commentary on the Book of Revelation* (Berrien Springs, MI: Andrews University Press, 2002), 313.

to be a very important person. Worship may mean giving a special greeting, respect, honor, or tribute. Sometimes we are deliberate about expressing worship and adoration toward human beings, but we are not so intentional about our respect and adoration toward the God who created us, holds our destiny in His hands, and deserves all of our worship. At one time, Paul and Barnabas healed a crippled man in Lystra. The local religious leaders were so amazed and overwhelmed by this miracle that they organized a ceremony to give worship to Paul and Barnabas as gods (Acts 14:8–18). The two missionaries were shocked and distressed; they utterly rejected that gesture with abject humility. They pointed to the God of the universe and implored all of the people present to worship only "the living God, who made the heaven, the earth, the sea, and all things that are in them" (Acts 14:15). Paul and Barnabas had an appropriate response. We must always direct people to worship God.

From ancient times, there have been examples of individuals who refused to ascribe worship to idols (Dan. 3:12–14) or to fellow human beings (Esther 3:2–5). In choosing to refuse worship to any but the Lord God, these followers risked their lives. They are given to us as worthy examples of fidelity. The final contest in the great controversy between good and evil will be about worship. Every person is called upon to show his or her true object of devotion. The two main contestants are God and the devil. Each of us must make a personal decision as to where we will place our allegiance. Worship does evince the differences between people. It shows where their hearts are inclined. God offers love, peace, and everlasting life, whereas the devil has hate, turmoil, lies, deception, and final death. It is always safe to remember the last call in Revelation 14:7. We would do well to worship God the Creator.

Final Call

Revelation 4 and 5 depict the glorious worship scene in heaven. God is acclaimed as "Holy, Holy, Holy, Lord God Almighty, who was and is and is to come" (Rev. 4:8). The heavenly throne is surrounded by worshipers who, in perfect unison, accentuate honor and praise to God. Jesus is the central figure on this magnificent occasion. He is acknowledged for the great salvation He worked out by dying for humanity. This grand worship experience is unique. It includes angels, as well as every creature in heaven and from everywhere else in the universe (Rev. 5:13). God is worshipped by His creatures. Bless the Lord. Oh, my soul!

As time runs out for people living on earth, God sends a special, final warning to help us get ready for transition to the heavenly Canaan. Just as Moses warned Israel at the border of the earthly Canaan that God alone should be worshipped in the Promised Land, God commissions His Church to summon the world to worship Him in the time of the end. Worship is one of those activities that we will continue even in the new heaven and new earth. The Church is commissioned to call all people back to worshipping God, the Creator. Such a timely message is in Revelation 14. It is best known as the three angels' messages, because the writer saw three angels flying in midair and calling out to people who live on earth. Jesus had already promised that the gospel of the kingdom of God would be preached to all the world, and then the end would come (Matt. 24:14). What we see in Revelation 14:6–7 is the announcement of the eternal gospel as a warning to those who dwell on earth. God, in His great mercy, warns us to be ready for the conclusion of our spiritual journey on earth.

The Bible declares,

> Then I saw another angel flying in the midst of heaven, having the everlasting gospel to preach to those who dwell on the earth—to every nation, tribe, tongue, and people—saying with a loud voice, "Fear God and give glory to Him, for the hour of His judgment has come; and worship Him who made heaven and earth, the sea and springs of water" (Rev. 14:6–7).

We see in this message that the messenger is flying above the earth. This signifies the speed and the urgency with which this message must be proclaimed. The recipients of the message are all of the people everywhere on the earth. The content of the message includes the call to fear God and give Him glory, the announcement of the judgment soon to be pronounced by God, the call to worship God, and affirmation of God's creatorship of everything in heaven and on earth.

Let me clarify the expression "fear God" in Revelation 14:7. The etymology of the word *fear*, understood from the Greek *phobeo* (verb) or *phobos* (noun), basically expresses two concepts in the Bible. Fear carries the sense of to be "afraid," "frightened," "terrified," or "alarmed," and also to "respect," "be in reverential fear," or "awe."[39] The fear of God is the basic element of the believer's faith. It is that reverential attitude we express in acknowledgment of the supremacy and sovereignty of God. When we fear God, we express our heartfelt confession, deep piety, worship, adoration, religious devotion, praise, honor, and commitment to God. By fearing God, we feel the evil of our behavior, we feel defiled of sin, and we feel unworthy of His grace and love. As a result, we confess our sin. We shun all evil. We fully surrender our life and let God take over and do His will in us. This is quite overwhelming to us as humans. Sometimes the spirit is willing, but the flesh objects to this. However, our love for our God will motivate us to yield completely to He who holds our destiny. This genuine desperation of a longing soul before the holy and glorious God receives transforming grace that helps us be godly. We then love God, keep His commandments, and do His divine will (John 14:15; John 15:10). We will obviously live upright to glorify God in our life. God calls us to fear Him, in the right way. The fear of God is the beginning of our wisdom (Job 28:28; Ps. 111:10; Prov. 1:7; Prov. 9:10). We shun evil and learn to depend on God all the time.

All world religions have gods. The people give offerings and sacrifices to these gods; they build temples and perform rituals. They observe festivals and special days; they fast and pray. Religions of the world teach about evil spirits and how to appease them or ward them off so that they will not cause harm. These religions also teach the concept of good and evil. The religions may have their own scripture or traditions. Religions teach about after life concepts. All religions worship. There is even devil worship. Surprisingly, many Christians perform worship activities for their God similar to those performed by other religions for their gods. The God who created heaven and earth and everything in them is to

---

[39] Mounce, *Mounce's Complete Expository Dictionary of Old and New Testament Words*, 244–245; Moulton, *The Analytical Greek Lexicon Revised*, 427–428.

be distinguished from any other thing revered or called god. The God of heaven and earth will not share His glory with things He has made (Isa. 42:8). God is a jealous God (Exod. 20:5) and will not accept worship from those who reverence any lesser thing.

Worship is absolutely reserved for God alone. Worshipping God as the Creator is the primary distinguishing mark between God and anything else humans would want to worship. We need to worship God in the way He wants us to worship Him, and at the time He chooses. It is appropriate to worship God every day of our life and wherever we happen to be. In spite of that, God has designated a special day, the Sabbath, on which worship is to take precedence over every other activity (Gen. 2:1–3; Exod. 20:3–11; Rev. 14:6–7). The time is now! God is looking for true worshipers who "will worship the Father in Spirit and truth; for the Father is seeking such to worship Him" (John 4:23).

When we worship God as Creator, we must do it properly. It is helpful to remember how it was in the beginning. The Bible declares, "Thus the heavens and the earth, and all the host of them, were finished. And on the seventh day God ended His work which He had done, and He rested on the seventh day from all His work which He had done. Then God blessed the seventh day and sanctified it, because in it He rested from all His work which God had created and made" (Gen. 2:1–3). God created everything in six literal days.[40]

On the seventh day, God rested. God blessed and sanctified the seventh day. He distinguished the seventh day of the week from all other days. This is the day designed for worship. This seventh day was marked in the context of creation. It is interesting to note the many Bible passages that call our attention to worship God as Creator (Exod. 20:3–11; Isa. 66:22–23; Acts 14:15; Rev. 14:6–7). These texts have something in common. God is Creator and must be worshipped by all His creation. Sabbath is the special day God designated for worship. Just prior the end of the world, there will be a contest between worshipping God on Saturday (biblical Sabbath) or on Sunday (the human traditional day for worship). We cannot ignore the seventh-day Sabbath if we truly worship God as Creator.

---

[40] There are several theories propounded on origins. True science gives more compelling and credible evidence for intelligent design.

Loud and clear, the second angel called, "Babylon is fallen, is fallen, that great city, because she has made all nations drink of the wine of the wrath of her fornication" (Rev. 14:8). This timely, universal message is a sequel to the previous one. It announces to the end-time people "the collapse of end-time Babylon, the worldwide apostate religious system and the confederacy of religious organizations backed by political powers of the world."[41] This message depicts the said religious system as a prostitute who seduces all nations to join in her fornication. This message is a warning to all people to not associate themselves with the corruption of this religious system.

The third angel augments the first two by announcing,

> If anyone worships the beast and his image, and receives *his* mark on his forehead or on his hand, he himself shall also drink of the wine of the wrath of God, which is poured out full strength into the cup of His indignation. He shall be tormented with fire and brimstone in the presence of the holy angels and in the presence of the Lamb. And the smoke of their torment ascends forever and ever; and they have no rest day or night, who worship the beast and his image, and whoever receives the mark of his name (Rev. 14:9–11).

Here is a clear call to worship the true God. Those who object to this become vulnerable to worshipping the beast and its image (Rev. 13). Such worshippers have no hope because they will face God's full judgment and final destruction.

There is a clear warning against associating with Babylon, the beast, and the image of the beast. Notice that all of the three angels' messages are addressed to everybody living at the time of the end. There are only two sides contesting for worship here: the choice is between God and anything else. Worship is solely reserved for God and nothing else. Through His great love, grace, and faithfulness, God invites us to show our allegiance to Him. He deserves all our devotion. Worship He who created! Worship God on His terms! It makes sense for anyone to

---

[41] Stefanovic, *Revelation of Jesus Christ*, 448.

worship the Creator rather than a thing created. We are grateful to God for giving us such a timely message so that we may escape into His great salvation. The call to worshipping God as Creator is a message of God's grace and His salvation.

I am looking forward to the time when all the redeemed of God from all over the earth will stand in adoration in His presence. In unison we will proclaim, "Salvation belongs to our God who sits on the throne, and to the Lamb!" (Rev. 7:10).

Chapter 5

DAUGHTERS ARE
CHILDREN TOO!

"IT'S HARD TO be a woman!" she sighed. The plight of women carves an indelible trail of pain down through human history. For the most part, ancient Near Eastern literature viewed "women as property and unnecessary"[42] or "merely as decorative—preoccupied with their physical charms."[43] Unfortunately, Israel's track record as the nation prepared to move into Canaan was still stained with discrimination against women. Five sisters, Mahlah, Noah, Hoglah, Milcah, and Tirzah (Num. 26:33) took this ugly problem to Moses (Num. 27:1–5). They were frustrated. Right there on the Plains of Moab, in the presence of Eleazar the priest, the leadership of the nation, and all of the people, the sisters made their complaint a public spectacle. As they shared their story, it became apparent that these sisters did not have a father, a brother, or any other close male relative to help them. They represented themselves.

The father of the five sisters was Zelophehad. He was from the tribe of Manasseh, the son of Joseph. Zelophehad's life ended at some point in the wilderness wanderings. The circumstances leading to his death are uncertain because the biblical record does not explain exactly what happened to him. His death could possibly be linked to the time when Korah died, along with some 250 rebels (Num. 16). According to the girls, Zelophehad was not numbered among the rebels but died "in his

---

[42] Jo Ann Davidson, "Women Bear God's Image: Considerations from a Neglected Perspective," *AUSS* 54 (2016), 34.
[43] Ibid., 37.

own sin" (Num. 27:3). His daughters did not elaborate on what caused their father's demise. Their point was that the death of their father was a major blow to them; it left them a vacuum that was never filled. They were left in an awkward position. Since his passing, they missed a father figure to guide them. He was never replaced by any of his tribesmen. He had neither son nor brothers.

Humans find it easy to complain about their predicaments and blame those who might have been responsible for their difficulties. Many people, both young and old, blame their parents for their difficult situations. They bewail their misfortune but do little or nothing to change the course of events in their lives. Instead of seeking to rectify their situations, they bemoan their plight and choose to play the victim, because the problems were created by their predecessors. In contrast, Zelophehad's five daughters chose not to waste time grumbling against the unfair social fabric or the legal problems. Instead, they took stock of their situation and began working toward a resolution. They were not going to sit idly by, moaning and complaining, while their father's posterity was left without any land or any remembrance in Canaan. They believed that they should have a place they could call home. They dared to think that something favorable could be worked out to solve the problem not only for themselves but also for those future women who might find themselves in a similar situation.

Many people in our contemporary world are trapped in ugly situations that are not of their own making. What we need today are people who think clearly about their awkward situations and take appropriate actions to resolve such untoward circumstances. People are needed today who will break the impasse and usher in change and new life in Christ.

Land Ownership

In that male-dominated community, it was critical for women to have male relatives who would represent them in all civil disputes. These five girls did not have any such representation. It must be noted that they stayed together and took care of each other despite their circumstances.

They never mention anything about their mother, so we do not know whether she was alive or dead. Even if she was alive, she could not help with the settlement problems the girls would face in Canaan. It is possible that the mother could have been the one to instigate this concern for the girls. She might have chosen to remain in the background. Mothers can be strong forces behind the scenes. Do not underestimate what a mother can do, either positively or negatively. Mothers are able engineers of social change. Whatever inspired this unusual assault against centuries of oppression, the five girls were alert and oriented. They understood very well what was going on. They were aware of the reason for the census that was going on among all the people.[44]

That census was for the purpose of land distribution (Num. 26:53). When everybody was talking about land allocation in Canaan, the girls became concerned. Their question was, "What about us?" They knew the law: no woman was allowed to own land. They would not have any part in the distribution unless they did something about it.

The daughters of Zelophehad were faced with a puzzling situation that could not be easily resolved by referring to any laws then in place. Men alone were counted in the census. Women were represented by the men who were related to them. The counted men were to receive the allocation of the land according to their tribal units (Num. 26:53). Zelophehad's daughters were faced with raising a question about women's rights without any male representation. There was no precedent to guide them in raising such a question, but it was of such pressing importance that they felt they must do something. Otherwise, where would they

---

[44] This is the second census on Israel (Num. 26). Some scholars have raised considerable concern over the statistics in the Exodus story and attempted to dismiss them as inflated (Exod. 12:37; Exod. 38:26; Num. 1:46; Num. 2:32; Num. 11:21; Num. 26:51). The numbers of the men eligible for war demand the whole nation to be at least two million people. Various ways of reading or emending the text have not been helpful. The numbers seem to be consistent with the text, which anticipates a remarkable growth of the population (Gen. 12:2; Gen. 15:5; Gen. 17:4–6; Gen. 22:17; Exod. 1:7, 9–10, 20). However, archaeological evidence on the Exodus story does not deny the possibility of such large numbers of people traversing the desert lands from Egypt to Canaan at that time. See Patrick Mazani, "The Number of Israelites at the Exodus Analyzed in the Light of Archaeology and Literary Evidence," MA Thesis, Andrews University, 1999.

live once they got into Canaan? They had to find a way to see whether something could be done.

Some legislation with regard land and property had already been put in place (Lev. 25:8–55). When legislation is in effect, it helps resolve some of the anomalies obtaining in the society. Although this may sound good, legislation is never fully comprehensive as long as humans live. Legislation has loopholes. There is always the possibility that something will come up that is not covered by the established legislation. This is the reason why laws are amended from time to time. Legislators try to accommodate unique situations that are not adequately addressed by existing laws. We hear talk about amending the amended amendment of the amended legislation. In this instance, the law for land distribution already in place had to be amended to accommodate the situation of these five ladies.

When the five daughters of Zelophehad gathered up their courage and appealed to Moses, he took their situation before the Lord, who told him to amend the existing law to allow the daughters of Zelophehad to own land (Num. 27:5–11). In the future, women in similar circumstances were also allowed to own land. However, this was not the end of the litigation. The tribesmen from Manasseh later approached Moses concerning the issue of females inheriting the land (Num. 36). Further inheritance problems surfaced showing that the new law still had an unfortunate loophole with regard to marriage and land possession. The issue of land ownership was settled appropriately on behalf of the five sisters, yet their kinsmen felt that the amendment would threaten loss of land for the whole tribe. The tribesmen reasoned that if the five daughters were married to men from different tribes, then their husbands would have the right to take the land from the women they married. The land would eventually belong to the tribes into which Zelophehad's daughters were married. If many of the daughters from the tribe of Manasseh got married all over the country, then the land for Manasseh would be taken over by the other tribes. In consideration of this legitimate complaint, the daughters of Zelophehad were instructed to confine their marriages to husbands who belonged to their father's tribe (Num. 36:6–9). If this second amendment became the standard for everybody, then marriage for girls in a situation similar to the five sisters would always be restricted to their own tribes.

The census established the fact that the tribe of Manasseh, son of Joseph, had 52,700 men who were able to go to war. It is very surprising that of all the thousands of men from Manasseh, the daughters of Zelophehad had no one to represent them. Among their own tribe, they had nobody. Imagine! Nobody for the girls, even though they were among their "father's brothers" (Num. 27:4).

Today, individualism is dominant. There are many people who feel alone when they are among their family members or fellow professionals. People feel as though they are alone while members in a church that has hundreds of believers. That aloneness may cause many to give up the struggle for life, especially if they are facing insurmountable problems. Many people drop out from their church families because they feel isolated, despite the numbers of believers around them. In some churches, there are individuals in whom nobody is interested. They have nobody who will get close to them or show interest in them as children of God. Such people can be lost right in the middle of a crowd of their peers.

A further point bears consideration here. Credulity would be stretched to the breaking point if we assumed that the daughters of Zelophehad were utterly incapable of establishing who, of all the thousands in their father's tribe, would be next of kin. However tragic the history of their near relatives, there had to be a male somewhere in the tribe who, though not "close," would be next of kin. Why did the daughters of Zelophehad not appeal to this person, who surely did exist? It is very possible that the sisters had good reason not to desire representation from the man or men who could have taken the place of next of kin. According to community practice, whoever was chosen to represent the five girls was also eligible for owning whatever land they could be allocated, as well as owning the girls themselves. These sisters presented their case and represented themselves because they did not want their father's land to be absorbed by whoever would claim it if they went to more distant next of kin. This point is very crucial. They wanted their father's name to be remembered, and they wanted to have something to say about whom they married and who obtained the land of their father. They came at the end of the wilderness journey and appealed to Moses as God's chosen leader. They wanted inheritance for themselves in the Promised Land, and God rewarded their appeal. Through Moses, God granted the request of the five sisters. From that day forward, women in similar circumstances would own land in Canaan.

It is true that the five sisters represented themselves with regard to material possessions, but there is a larger lesson here. What I take from the example of these young ladies is that there are some important matters in which we do not want any available representation. With regard to inheriting eternal life, each person has to represent himself or herself before God. No one is going to be saved because of the righteousness of a family member (Ezek. 14:14). With regard to our own salvation, we need to present ourselves to Jesus now, before we cross over into the Promised Land. The time to obtain reservations for our heavenly mansion is now! It is on an individual basis.

Law Amendment

The Zelophehad sisters found their way to Moses and lodged their complaint. Moses had no idea how to solve the case. Fortunately, Moses knew what to do in such a situation. As a seasoned leader, the best thing he could do was to take the complex issue to God. Leaders do well if they take unclear issues to God in prayer. There are many issues that are not clearly addressed in the Bible or any other inspired sources. Leaders blunder if they rationalize on such issues without taking time to consult God.

Notice that the daughters of Zelophehad came at the end of the journey. Likewise, as God's people approach the time of the end, they will face many issues concerning women that are not clearly defined, even in the Bible. Such issues are brought before Church leaders for consideration. Even believers who are leaders may blunder if they adopt sociological methods or follow cultural trends to resolve theological cases. Theological issues are best resolved theologically. Spiritual things are spiritually discerned (1 Cor. 2:14). The issue with the five girls was a theological matter because it was God who directed the distribution of the land (Num. 26:52–53). God started the whole issue, and He had to deal with the anomalies and come up with an amicable solution. It is God alone who can interpret what He himself has established. If an exception is to be granted, it is God alone who can grant it. If God does not see fit to make a change in what He stated before, then it is safe to abide by the light God has given us on the subject.

In the case of Zelophehad's daughters, God consented to the request for an exception. In fact, God said that they were "right" in what they requested (Num. 27:7). The granted request was also to accommodate any similar situation that might be encountered in the future. What a breakthrough! Under certain circumstances, women can own land in Canaan. The case of the five sisters has been brought up by many who point out that God consented to a request presented before Him with regard to the modification of an established law. Many people today question why gay marriages cannot be acceptable when God consented to the request of the five sisters. God did not intend the issue of Zelophehad's daughters to be the model for settling all problems believers encounter at the end of time. Not every issue we bring to God at the end of time may be granted. It is irresponsible theology to assume that because God accepted the five sisters' request, He will concede on every issue we want. We must not cherish the idea that because one group's request led to the amendment of certain legislation, it necessarily follows that we can assume that change will be granted in our situation. God reserves the right to judge each situation according to His divine principles, and it behooves human beings to accept His judgments.

There are clear guidelines in the Bible, and these guidelines must be followed with regard to our wishes. It is vitally important to cherish the guidelines God has given to us. If there is enough light on any subject, then the best thing we can do is to abide by that guidance. If there is no light at all from the inspired sources we have, then we should be very careful not to forge our own path without God's consent. We should be especially careful in regard to things that we think do not pertain to our salvation. If we rationalize about issues on which the Bible does not give clear guidance, we are likely bound to move in a direction where God is not. When unclear issues come up, the Church should prayerfully seek God for solutions. To our finite, human minds, it may seem that some problems in our own setting may be alleviated by choosing to change the precedents God has given. But if God does not sanction our proposed solution, we place ourselves in a fatal fault. We should never use one passage of scripture to override other clear passages when we make any crucial decision for the believers. Neither should we misuse scripture to support what we want, despite its context. Eisegesis is the interpretation of a text by reading into it our own ideas. This method of study leads to dangerous conclusions.

Backed up by Men

One of the customary laws given to Israel during their journeying toward the Promised Land dealt with a vow or commitment made by women. This law stated that if any woman makes a personal resolution and vows to do something voluntarily, what she decided to do would be binding and an inviolable oath as long as some men of the family heard what she said and remained quiet about it (Num. 30). If the father, husband, or any male relative overheard the woman pledging a vow for the Lord, and objected to it at that time, then the woman was not required to follow through with her commitment; the vow would be thus nullified. In other words, women were not independent in making their own vows to God. A man had to validate it. Not so for men. A man could resolve to do a certain thing, and he did not need any audience to bind himself to a personal commitment. Unfortunately, there were no ladies in Israel at that time who stood up to challenge this regulation in a way similar to the challenge the daughters of Zelophehad brought with regard to land ownership.

In many different parts of the world today, women are not allowed the privilege to make important personal decisions. Some customary laws still bind women captive among their own people. In some societies, a woman who rejects an arranged marriage and decides to choose for herself one whom she wants to marry can be killed for her decision. This is a painful reality that many women are facing today.

Ancient Laws Regarding Land Possession

In ancient Mesopotamia, there were many laws that had to do with land possession. Gudea (2150 BC) reports on a cylinder, "In a house that had no male heir, he installed its daughter as heir."[45] Hammurabi (ca. 1792–1750 BC) established some laws that had also to do with land administration. Law 29 stated that the son of a captured soldier should be given his father's land and orchard.[46] If the son was too young, then one-third of the land and orchard would be given to the son's mother. Law 150 stated that if a man makes a sealed document for his wife to get the field, orchard, house, or moveable property after his death, it shall not be contested by anyone, even his own children.[47]

Moses, informed by God in the second millennium BC, established some land acquisition laws for women in Israel (Num. 27:1–11; Num. 36:1–13). Therefore we see that women in the ancient past were able to acquire land under special circumstances.

The book of Job talks about Jemimah, Keziah, and Keren-Happuch (Job 42:13–15). These were the three daughters whom God gave to Job after his fiery ordeal. No women around them were as beautiful as these three. The Bible states that Job, their father, gave his three daughters inheritance, property, or possession along with their seven brothers. The Hebrew word *naḥălâ*, used in Job 42:15 for inheritance, is the same word used over and over again with regard to Israel getting the land of Canaan (Deut. 4:38; Deut. 15:4). It is therefore possible that the daughters of Job might have owned some land among their brothers. Women in the ancient past were land owners. God allowed women in Israel to own land because it was an acceptable practice. In the New Testament, the Christian will inherit the kingdom of God in Christ (Eph. 1:11; Rom. 8:17).

The Voice of Women

The French Revolution (1789–1799) was marked by radical social upheaval, religious tensions, changes in economic trends, technological advancement, and political rebellion that challenged the way things had been. It also brought in new ways of viewing life. The influence of this

---

[45] *COS*, 2:432, Cylinder B xviii, lines 8–9.
[46] Ibid., 2:338.
[47] Ibid., 2:345.

enlightenment movement has since spread all over the world. Although it has had a major impact on civilizing our world, there is still more to work on in our contemporary society.

Several organizations have been created in an attempt to address the social ills in our society. These include workers' unions in industry, students' unions at the tertiary level, civil rights movements, human rights, women's rights, and the like. Even though the approach is political, these groups are consistently addressing social ills everywhere, even at the doorstep of the Church. The fight is against discrimination or stigmatization of any nature toward anyone. The activists call for equal opportunities in all spheres of life, whether secular or religious, liberal or conservative. Thousands of international organizations to empower women have been put in place. Slogans like "Women rights are human rights" get out the message. There are so many projects aiming to raise community awareness on violence against women.

This revolution has affected all facets of human existence. Many changes have been made, and changes will continue to the very end of time. We acknowledge that the world has since become a better place to live through some of the changes. At the same time, the world is also suffering much from some of the effects of ill-conceived changes that have been put in place.

Some of the major changes the world has experienced since the French Revolution have to do with women in the society. We can easily call this the rise of women. Serious changes in favor of women have been effected in a number of countries. The ancient world was male dominated. The inequalities that existed between men and women have been violently attacked. The new era demanded no preferential treatment for men. Several areas in life were impacted, and some of the inequities spawned by gender preference have been successfully excised. Women can pursue education in whatever field of study they prefer. They can rise to whatever position they wish to attain. They can take up the career of their choice without discrimination. Women can contest for child custody. They can acquire and dispose of property. In many countries, women are eligible to fully participate in politics and the voting process. They can contest for any political position and can even be national leaders. Women are accepted into the army, and some of the privileges they wish to enjoy there are currently being assessed. Women can draw legal contracts. They can own property or become entrepreneurs. Married women can get top executive jobs, and in turn their husbands may choose to be full-time dads at home.

The rise of women to occupy positions where men had previously dominated has not been an easy struggle. Some of our contemporary nations have difficulties in accepting this social reality. In many countries of the world today, women have been liberated to occupy places that were previously held by men alone. This is not true everywhere. There are still some discrepancies in remuneration, even in countries that seem to support the rise of women. In some cases, men are still being paid higher wages than women for the same job. In many parts of the world, sports that are more physically demanding have been played only by men because women have been far outmatched by the men. Women have generally had little chance of winning unless competing against other women. This explains the reason why we still have Olympics for men and women separately.

We should not forget the fact that God made humans "male and female" (Gen. 1:27). Even though women have been labeled "weaker vessels," husbands are encouraged to love their wives because they are "heirs together of the grace of life" (1 Pet. 3:7). Our gender roles are complimentary. We do well to keep our gender differences distinct because they are God-given. Men and women need each other. Women and their advocates have spoken out against unfair male domination and marginalization. We still see demonstrations on women issues in the streets. There is still more work to be done in favor of women today, and at the same time we would do well to make sure that their lot is truly improved and not changed for the worse. God made men and women with valuable differences, and erasing these differences in the name of equality is not an improvement for anyone.

The fight for equality between men and women has broadened in unexpected ways. There is a growing feverish excitement in our contemporary world about those who choose to be transgender. A transgender individual claims a different gender than the one with which he or she was born. Many such individuals go for medical assistance to transition from one gender to another. There are also some individuals who are born with physical features not exclusively masculine or feminine. Such people have been labeled genderqueer, bigender, pangender, genderfluid, gender-neutral, agender, transgender, gender-non-conforming (GNC), and so on. Whatever our physical situation, the question is, "Will the thing formed say to him who formed it, 'Why have you made me like this?'" (Rom. 9:20; Isa. 29:16; Isa. 45:9).

Feminist Approaches to the Bible

There has been some significant progress in "liberating" women in the secular world. More recently, an effort is being put forth to effectively understand the Bible with regard to the role of women. This effort is now known as feminist hermeneutics. Basically, feminist hermeneutics is an intellectual critique of masculine "superiority" in the Bible. This movement has been understood as a "theoretical exploration of biblical interpretation in the interest of women."[48] This kind of scholarship observes that the Bible was written by men and for men. The evidence cited is the masculine language the Bible uses. As a result, those who advocate for this trend of thought attempt to remove from the Bible all masculine terms and replace them with generic terms inclusive of women. Words like female, femaleness, human, humane, humanitarian, humanity, humankind, humanly, humanness, kinsman, kinsmen, manhandle, mankind, manmade, manslaughter, manslayer, woman, womanhood, womanhouse, and women, are thought to be problematic because they have "male" and "man/men" in them. Such words do not make feminists happy. It must be pointed out that the feminism that is stirring up so much publicity is actually being promoted by a small, elite minority in the academic community, as well as in some Church circles. Its interpretive methodology is inspired by contemporary politics.

Feminists try to interpret the Bible politically, scientifically, and sociologically in order to redress the cultural and linguistic issues that they choose to understand as biased toward men. They have pressured biblical scholars to come up with a biblical text that is more gender sensitive. The feminist reader resists biblical expressions that depict

---

[48] Elisabeth Schüssler Fiorenza, "Feminist Hermeneutics," *ABD* (1992), 2:784.

women as submissive, dependent, or inferior to men. In extreme cases, these feminists go so far as to make some of their texts address God as female. The third-person masculine pronouns in the Bible are displaced by neutral ones. The latest versions of the Bible change the pronouns dealing with God to make them gender neutral rather than perpetuating the generic masculine expressions that were representative of both genders. A good example of this is Matthew 10:40, "He who receives you receives Me, and he who receives Me receives Him who sent Me" (NKJV). Today's New International Version (TNIV) renders this same verse as, "Anyone who welcomes you welcomes me, and anyone who welcomes me welcomes the one who sent me." In this particular case TNIV presents the text more accurately than other translations, and this is a positive development to the text. However, neutralizing gender in most of the biblical passages robs scripture of its authoritative aura. We acknowledge that language has gone through many changes. Words can change their meaning. We also have new vocabulary coming in almost every day. Yet the literal meaning of the original biblical text must not be sacrificed for any political or social agenda.

The feminist goal is a biblical text that eradicates the male-dominant language and renders the text more gender sensitive. It is true that both women and men are equals before God. But these gender-neutral Bibles often depict God Himself as gender neutral. Feminism, along with some elements of liberation theology, demand women's emancipation from male dominance in all spheres of life. Women are encouraged to be what they want to be. People who want to be politically correct now read the older versions of the Bible by adding "or she" where the Bible has the generic "he." Accurate translations of the Bible do contain many instances where metaphor and simile compare aspects of God's character with female characteristics, but these do not give credence to the idea that God is female, as some feminists would like to believe (see Num. 11:12; Deut. 32:18; Job 38:8, 29; Ps. 131:2; Isa. 42:14; Isa. 46:3–4; Isa. 49:14–15; Isa. 66:12–13; Hosea 11:1–4; Acts 17:28; 1 Pet. 2:2–3).

Some women have been very vocal about their unfortunate treatment by men in all spheres of life. They have cried incessantly for equality with men in church leadership. This is a very thorny issue that has torn apart denominations and forced some churches to close down for failing to reach a resolution regarding this matter. The difficulty seems to arise from the silence of scripture on whether or not women should be in headship positions. It has not been easy for the Church to come to a consensus on how to settle this issue. Despite this, the voice of women and their supporters has not been in vain. Women have been appointed leaders at all levels in some religious traditions. Women are counted among the clergy. There are now female priests in some religious circles. The number of ordained women in ministry is on the rise in the contemporary Christian churches. Traditional views and cultural norms have been demolished to accommodate gender equality at all hierarchical ecclesiastical levels.

The voice of women has done much to transform the social landscape. But feminists have not yet accomplished everything they envisioned to be necessary before they are satisfied. Those advocating for women's liberation have come at just the time they might have been expected: the time of the end. Just as the Zelophehad sisters rose up at the end of Israel's earthly journey, we see that some women also at this time of the end are speaking out on issues that pertain to them. These issues are coming just before the saints' transition into the heavenly Canaan. What we should notice, however, is that today's women are calling for concerns that pertain to this side of heaven. Zelophehad sisters pleaded for inheritance when they crossed over. Unlike these five sisters, those who advocate for women's rights want their earthly share now. They want the inequalities addressed before Jesus comes. They are calling for their fair share not in heaven but on earth. Heaven will be different. There is no sin there. There is no unfairness there. There is no one dominant over the other.

We see that women are voicing all kinds of different concerns in these last days. Many of their concerns are legitimate. Women have suffered much under the tyranny of men, and they need a break. They need security. Many things that women are calling for seem to be reasonable, such as receiving their fair and equal payment for work equal to that of men. Unfortunately, Galatians 3:28 has been brutally misused to make a case for equality of women and men in all spheres of life. The context of the text is clear: that we do not have distinction when we are in Christ. The text is not abolishing being male or being female. It is not abolishing the roles God designated at creation when He made the man and the woman. It is not good biblical scholarship that wrests scripture to erase all distinctions between women and men. At the same time, it is a crime before God for men to mistreat women or assume priority status over women.

Women's Issues at the End of Time

One may ask, "What are the issues women should raise as the world comes to an end?" This is too broad a question. To answer in short: Women are facing a plethora of issues to deal with. Many women face injustices in every sphere of life; we cannot comprehensively catalogue here everything that adversely affects them. Throughout history, women have resisted exploitation by men. This seems to be the central issue. In the last few years, we have seen the social landscape transformed by the emancipation of women. There are many secular and religious organizations that operate solely to alleviate the problems women are facing today. These organizations have made life much more bearable for many women. Some of the fastest-growing criminal activities today are drug trafficking, human trafficking, labor trafficking and sex trafficking. Slavery has not been completely exterminated. Mostly, girls and young women are trapped in these evil practices. Much effort is being put in place internationally to stop these dehumanizing and traumatizing activities.

Some "advances" have not been such a blessing. Persons of both genders are now free to choose the gender they want. There are men who make themselves look like women and are now called by female names. On the other hand, some women have gone for genetic alteration, and they now wear a beard, talk or dress like men, and show masculine features. They are called by male names. These women can legally become husbands to other women. As a couple, they can adopt children so as to establish a family of their own. The irony is that whereas some women fight for equality with men, others want to behave and look like men. The issue of transgender persons is gaining ground. The demand is launched for bisexual or all-gender facilities in schools and other public places. Men and women, and even young children, are going for transgender identities. A vocal minority is demanding the right to be classified as male or female based on their chosen identification.

There are a very few people who actually might have been born with ambiguous genitalia. These cannot be easily classified as male or female, but as intersex. Such individuals may align themselves with either gender depending on their preference or on the higher percentage of their maleness or femaleness in their physical makeup. For some, birth certificates are now filled "intersex," where it is supposed to be male or female. Those who advocate for transgender rights often use individuals with ambiguous genitalia as an excuse, but most of those choosing to re-identify as a different gender have no such excuse.

At the last camp of Israel before getting into Canaan, we notice that some women presented their concerns regarding inheritance to Moses. The issue did not become a movement affecting all Israelite women. Most of the women were content with their situation. The issue raised by the Zelophehad sisters was specific to daughters whose fathers were dead and who had no brothers to take over the property and carry on the family name. It did not concern all of the women in Israel, even though it became a national issue. We see that the daughters of Zelophehad did not want someone else to inherit land on their behalf; they wanted to inherit the land for themselves. At the end of time, some women activists will stand up for their rights. They will not tolerate what they consider to be the role of second-class citizens.

However, many women do not want to be identified with those who choose to fight for their own rights. Many women embrace specific changes that they feel do not conflict with their faith and conventional practice. They reject those changes that threaten their relationship with God and with other people. Care must be exercised by Church leaders when addressing women's concerns that are not clearly specified in the Bible. We must not be influenced by social pressure, politics, or psychology to make decisions that are not backed by the light God has given us in His Word. Church-based women's ministries offer ardent support to women for spiritual growth, as well as meeting their personal, multicultural, and multiethnic needs. Women are a vital component of the Church. Their remarkable contributions and service help to build and sustain our communities. Women of faith, prayer, vision, and commitment are Church assets to reckon with in this time of the end. Women of sanctified ingenuity build families, transform societies, and contribute to God's work while inspiring others with hope in the coming of Jesus. There are many women who are not driven by the demands of contemporary pressure. These encourage other women to seek to be what God wants them to be. The call is extended to all women, younger and older: "The time is ripe for a new movement—a seismic holy quake of countercultural Christian women who dare to take God at His Word, who have the courage to stand against the popular tide, choosing to believe and delight in God's plan for male and female."[49]

On matters pertaining to survival in this current world, men should not deter women from making use of their God-given potential. Men should not block women's path to salvation, because daughters are God's children too! Let the men encourage the daughters to serve the Lord according to scriptural wisdom so that they will not be wholly engrossed with the things of the world. Daughters must plead with God on their own behalf for their heavenly inheritance.

---

[49] Mary A. Kassian, "You've Come a Long Way, Baby!" in *Voices of the True Woman Movement*, ed. Nancy Leigh DeMoss (Chicago: Moody Publishers, 2010), 70.

Chapter 6

QUALIFIED BY THE SPIRIT

MOSES LEARNED FROM God that his fate was sealed and that he could not go into Canaan. Like many others, he had rebelled against God's orders on the journey from Egypt to the Promised Land (Exod. 17:7; Num. 20:7–13). Once Moses realized that God was not going to change His mind about refusing him entrance to Canaan, he petitioned God to choose someone else who was qualified to lead the people across the Jordan. Even though the people were ready to go into the land of promise, they still needed spiritual and secular leadership. Leadership will also be necessary as God's people at the end of time prepare to go over into the heavenly Canaan. Wherever there is a group of people, leadership is necessary to plan, guide, encourage, inspire, support, lead, and maintain unity. Spiritual leadership calls for a visionary who will prayerfully exploit opportunities to glorify God among believers.

Many people fail to think of preparing a successor while they are still leading out. These fail to make sure that there is someone to carry on when they are gone. A good and wise leader will have a deliberate plan to groom others who will then be ready to take over when the first leader lays aside the mantle of responsibility. Political leaders who do not want to give up their positions resist the idea of preparing a successor. They seem to think that they can stay in their positions forever, and they often resort to wicked schemes to maintain their leadership roles. Many times these long-serving leaders become dictators. A leader should never feel indispensable. The good of the people should be more important than the position.

In local churches, there are people who have served in leadership positions for many years. The contributions of long-serving leaders are often tremendous and should be appreciated. However, some of these well-meaning, long-serving leaders fail to think of the needs of the Church once they must step aside. They believe they are doing God's will and are not inclined to prepare others to take their places. To replace such leaders is sometimes a struggle for the local church. Effective leaders should pave the way for others to take over when they leave office. They should make sure that passing the baton will be seamless and immediately effective. The best leaders are those who have learned to be good followers.

Moses was a wise leader. For many years, he had been keeping some individuals close as apprentices, preparing them for leadership roles. Ever since Israel had left Egypt, God's chosen leader was preparing others to carry the burden of leadership. He was confident that there were those who could readily assume the leadership when it was time for him to step down. But Moses wanted to make sure that the next leader was chosen not by man, but by God.

God's people were coming to the end of their long journey. They were about to cross into the land God had promised to their ancestors. Despite Israel's proximity to Canaan, leadership was still important to guide the nation in possessing and developing the land. Without leadership, everything would be chaotic; Israel would pour cross the Jordan and scatter themselves in total disarray. The strongest would take the best plots of ground, and the rest would drop down on any space they could find and defend. If they were a disorderly company, they could easily fall prey to the Canaanites. Therefore God instructed Moses to take Joshua to be his successor.

Joshua was the son of Nun and was from the tribe of Ephraim (Num. 13:8). Manasseh and Ephraim were the two sons of Joseph in Egypt. Grandfather Jacob blessed Ephraim, Joseph's younger son, and gave Ephraim precedence over his older brother, Manasseh (Gen. 48:5–20). The preference of Ephraim over his brother may have paved the way for his descendent, Joshua, to assume leadership of the nation. Joshua had long been an outstanding assistant to Moses in dealing with the people. The people knew Joshua, and Joshua knew the people. More important, Joshua knew the God of Moses—the God of Abraham and Isaac and

Jacob. This God was Joshua's God, and he knew how to take his orders from God.

Joshua's Qualification for Leadership

Joshua is first introduced when Moses entrusted him to fight with the Amalekites at Rephidim (Exod. 17:8–9). Moses told Joshua to choose able men and take them to fight the Amalekites. Moses chose to watch the conflict from the top of a hill while Joshua and his contingent battled the enemy on the plains below. The record of this encounter says that Joshua defeated the enemy. The Lord then told Moses to write about the battle and keep a record of it. Moses was also instructed by God to recite to Joshua the words he wrote about this historical battle (Exod. 17:14). It was an occasion of significance to Joshua and to all of Israel. It must not be left without a memorial. God wanted to make sure that Joshua would remember in the future that God would destroy Amalek from the face of the earth. It seems that at that time, Joshua was already being primed for leadership.

On another important occasion, Joshua was seen in the company of Moses, a group of priests, and seventy elders of Israel. They all went up into a mountain at God's invitation. Moses then left the elders and priests and took only Joshua with him when God called him to go up higher on the mountain. At this time, Joshua was introduced as Moses's attendant (Exod. 24:13). He became known by this designation (Exod. 33:11; Num. 11:28). Of the whole group that went up the mountain with Moses, Joshua was the only one allowed to accompany Moses when he came close to God. Even Joshua was left a little way behind when Moses was finally called to approach God and receive the Ten Commandments written on stone (Exod. 24:15–18). There on Mount Sinai, Joshua stood second only to Moses, who physically came into the presence of God. Joshua was the first person to see Moses carrying the Ten Commandments after he received them from the hand of God. Of all the children of Israel, Joshua alone was privileged to be an eyewitness to the close relationship God had with Moses. Joshua was allowed to see God's face-to-face meetings with Moses (Exod. 33:11).

Joshua was not very old when Moses started grooming him for leadership, but Moses discerned the promise in this fine young man. Every leader, and every human being, has a dark side. The scriptures show us the other side of the man Joshua. Moses had summoned seventy elders to come and meet with the Lord at the entrance of the Tabernacle. The Lord took some of the power of the Spirit that was in Moses and spread it among the seventy elders. All of these leaders began prophesying. It was immediately reported that two of the elders, Eldad and Medad, were prophesying in the camp, but they were not among those who had come to the meeting. Joshua, who had been Moses's aide since youth, spoke up against the two men and asked Moses to stop them. Much to Joshua's surprise, Moses rebuked him for being jealous. In fact, Moses said that he wished that all of God's people were prophets (Num. 11:24–30). It seems that Joshua must have accepted the rebuke of Moses with meekness.

At some time early on in their journey from Egypt to Canaan, before the forty years of wandering in the desert, Joshua and eleven others were sent on a mission to spy out the land of Canaan (Num. 13:8). It was on this occasion that Moses gave his assistant *Hoshea*, "salvation," the name *Yehoshua* (Joshua), "the Lord saves/delivers" (Num. 13:16; 1 Chron. 7:27).[50] This foreshadows Joshua as a deliverer of God's people from their enemies. It also portends his calling to lead them into Canaan. The meaning of the name *Joshua* is the equivalent of the New Testament name *Jesus* (Matt. 1:21). Each of the twelve men chosen to spy out the land was a leading representative of his tribe. Of these twelve spies, it was Joshua and Caleb who came back with a positive report (Num. 14:6–10). Even in his youth, Joshua evinced the optimism of a seasoned leader. He fully envisioned the possibility of overcoming obstacles to occupy the land that God had promised.

A godly leader faces the problems inherent in any great undertaking with courage because he operates not in his own strength, but in the mighty power of God. Such a spiritual leader visualizes the unlimited possibilities resident in God's intervention. Joshua fully trusted God's involvement in ousting the nations which occupied Canaan. His daring

---

[50] *NIDOTTE*, 4:808.

confidence, energized by his faith in God and motivated by the abilities potential in Israel, proved him a visionary leader. Joshua had shared some leadership responsibilities with Moses through the years. Under God, he had successfully led the army of Israel against the Amalekites at Rephidim (Exod. 17:8–13). He worked closely with, and unwaveringly supported Moses at all times. He had been to the mountaintop with Moses when Moses received the Ten Commandments. He showed his ardent commitment to God and to His mission to lead Israel into Canaan. Joshua demonstrated the vision, fidelity, commitment, and hope that God would use to successfully lead Israel to their destination. He believed in the God who completes His assignments and fulfills His promises.

Joshua comes into his leadership role at the time when Israel was completing the dreary, forty-year journey from Egypt to Canaan. God had the right individual for the task at hand; he had been rightly trained by God and Moses. This was the man through whom God would demonstrate His providence and protection to Israel.

As we come to the end of time, God will work with leaders whose daring trust in God will inspire believers to be ready for their transition into eternal life. In the end-time, the Church needs leaders who will champion God's truth in the face of seemingly impossible circumstances. They will lead out in obeying God's orders with a confidence born of faith. Leaders who are true, honest, and spiritual will safely navigate the difficult times by keeping the Church together and focused on the coming of the Savior. Leaders who are sensitive to the promptings of the Holy Spirit are an asset in the Church that is waiting for the soon return of Jesus.

Joshua was from the tribe of Joseph through Ephraim. Joseph had made Israel to move away from the land of promise. They went into Egypt for survival (Gen. 45:9–11). Four hundred and thirty years later (Exod. 12:40),[51] Joshua, a descendent of Joseph, led Israel back into the land of promise (Josh. 3, 4).[52] The remains of Joseph were brought back

---

[51] See chapter 1, footnote 2.

[52] A similar analogy is put forward by Bernard White, who writes that "the names of Adam and Joshua are typologically suggestive, particularly when considering as starting and ending points. It was Adam who (unwittingly) led God's first children

into Canaan by one of his descendents (Gen. 50:26; Exod. 13:19). This return of the remains of Joseph signifies the truth that when God's end-time people cross over into the heavenly Canaan, God will not forget those faithful ones who have died in anticipation of His deliverance from this sinful world. Joseph was not resurrected from death when he was carried back into Canaan, but we know that the righteous dead will be resurrected at the sound of the last trumpet. This is what Daniel 12:2 is referring to when it says that those who sleep in the dust shall awake. In 1 Thessalonians 4:14–17, it becomes clear that when Jesus returns, the dead in Christ shall rise first. Then the righteous people still living at that time shall be caught up together with them to meet the Lord in the air.

The Bible says that Joseph had the Spirit of God in him (Gen. 41:38). Similarly, Joshua's appointment as leader of Israel was based upon the fact that he had the Spirit of God in him (Num. 27:18). Those appointed by God to leadership positions will be people who are filled with His Holy Spirit. Leadership is safe only when one is fully open to the Holy Spirit. By the same token, "there is no limit to the usefulness of the one who, putting self aside, makes room for the working of the Holy Spirit upon his heart, and lives a life wholly consecrated to God."[53] Being Spirit filled was Joshua's primary qualification for taking over from Moses. Such leaders can accomplish great exploits for God. A Spirit-filled man will discern spiritual matters spiritually (1 Cor. 2:14). He will seek to glorify God in decision-making and in carrying out God's business. God has work for a person who is filled with the Holy Spirit.

Joshua's Appointment

The responsibility for choosing leaders in the Old Testament remained with God alone. God chose the prophets, priests, kings, and certain other individuals for specific assignments. God determined the Levitical

---

out of paradise; it was Joshua's life work to lead them into Canaan, the land where God would establish His name and where His presence would abide." See "Adam to Joshua: Tracing a Paragenealogy," *AUSS* 54 (2016), 24.

[53] Ellen G. White, *Christian Service* (Hagerstown, MD: Review and Herald Publishing Association, 1925), 254.

priesthood (Num. 3). Obviously, God chose Moses to deliver Israel from Egypt. Even though Moses had groomed Joshua, Moses appealed to God to choose his successor (Num. 27:16). It is difficult to know today the extent to which God is involved in the appointment of our leaders. In both the secular and religious spheres, the process for selecting leaders is characterized by humans who seek to consolidate power by fighting, scheming, and manipulating. The process is different today, but true leaders must still be appointed by God. The wisdom of heaven must, in spite of human meddling, initiate and confirm the call to those whom God has chosen for ministry. Once nominated by God, the leader is equipped with the abilities necessary as tools for the trade.

As Moses contemplated his impending death, he talked with God about Israel's need of a qualified leader. Without such, Israel would be "like sheep which have no shepherd" (Num. 27:17). Where there are human beings, leadership is imperative. The Lord told Moses to appoint Joshua, the son of Nun, who had shown outstanding commitment to God and exceptional leadership skills. Specifically, God pointed out the preeminent qualification in Joshua. He was "a man in whom is the Spirit" (Num. 27:18). Being a man of the Spirit becomes the prerequisite qualification for anyone who would take any office for God. Joshua was appointed to office not merely because of his lineage, but because he was qualified for the post based on his spirituality and personal experience. At this point in time, God's believers are waiting to cross into eternity. God still wants to ordain leaders whose lives give evidence that the Spirit of God is in them. God will use such leaders to rally His people for the final events of this world's history.

Joshua's Inauguration

The new leader of Israel, Joshua, the son of Nun, had worked for many years as Moses's right-hand man. He had proved himself worthy of the confidence placed in him. The Lord told Moses to initiate Joshua into his new position. The inauguration ceremony took place in the presence of the priest Eleazar and the entire congregation of Israel. Moses laid his hands on Joshua. In fact, the Hebrew word used in Numbers 27:18,

23 and Deuteronomy 34:9 is *sāmak*, "lean upon, lay, put, rest, uphold, support."[54] This word is used in the laying of hands. It is noted that "in the Levitical regulations regarding the sacrificial offerings, the offerer brought his proper sacrificial animal in person and laid his hand upon its head, thus expressing identification with the offering, its surrender to God and in the case of guilt, its transfer to the animal."[55]

Note that in Numbers 27:18, the hand is singular, but in Numbers 27:23 and Deuteronomy 34:9, Moses lays both hands. In Numbers 27:18, the hand is singular, stating an instructive principle. In Numbers 27:23 and Deuteronomy 34:9, the hands are plural, indicating the practice in fact. The laying of hands on a newly appointed leader implies support and encouragement, as well as transference of authority to that individual.[56] Laying hands on a designated candidate signifies being consecrated and dedicated to the service of the Lord. The ordained individual is separated from the ordinariness of life to a meaningful spiritual realm ratified by the presence of the Holy Spirit. Such a person should always be obedient to the promptings of the Holy Spirit, and in this he glorifies God.

The ordination of Joshua was no secret to the people. Moses conducted the inauguration service publicly as the Lord had directed him. On this occasion, Moses conferred some of his authority *(hôdh)* to Joshua (Num. 27:20). *Hôdh* means "splendor, majesty, authority, vigor." This transfer by Moses to Joshua implies the sharing of "any good quality or endowment for which a person is admired, honoured, or praised."[57] So Moses secured the respect he had previously received from the people to his successor. The giving of partial authority to Joshua may have some theological significance (see Num. 11:25). Moses empowered Joshua, not to be his duplicate, but to be an independent individual with whom God would work. What Joshua received from Moses was sufficient for him to get started. He was supposed to grow on his own to realize his full potential. Leaders are not given all they need at the onset; they develop their skills as their faith grows.

---

54 *BDB*, 701; *TWOT*, 2:628.

55 *TWOT*, 2:628.

56 *NIDOTTE*, 3:270–271.

57 William Wilson, *Old Testament Word Studies* (Grand Rapids: Kregel, 1978), 221.

By laying hands on Joshua, Moses publicly declared Joshua's divine appointment to all of Israel. As the people witnessed the ordination, they were obligated to respect and obey Joshua just as they had respected and obeyed Moses. Joshua now had full juridical authority over the nation. However, he was to work hand in hand with the priestly office. Deuteronomy 34:9 reports on the investiture of Joshua into his leadership role. Joshua was "full of the spirit of wisdom" because Moses had, under the guidance of God, laid hands on him. Now, wisdom in the Old Testament has a wide range of meanings. It is not only limited to genius, skill, shrewdness, or prudence; wisdom also includes "technical expertise and other professional capabilities of various types."[58] Wisdom enables one to distinguish between good and evil so as to render correct judgment. Biblical wisdom always originates from God (Prov. 1:7; Prov. 2:6; James 1:5–6). Anything apart from God is foolishness.

God empowered Joshua for service. When Moses was off the scene, God came to the newly appointed Joshua and assured him of His support. God said to Joshua,

> Moses My servant is dead. Now therefore, arise, go over this Jordan, you and all this people, to the land which I am giving to them—the children of Israel. Every place that the sole of your foot will tread upon I have given you, as I said to Moses. From the wilderness and this Lebanon as far as the great river, the River Euphrates, all the land of the Hittites, and to the Great Sea toward the going down of the sun, shall be your territory. No man shall *be able to* stand before you all the days of your life; as I was with Moses, *so* I will be with you. I will not leave you nor forsake you. Be strong and of good courage, for to this people you shall divide as an inheritance the land which I swore to their fathers to give them. Only be strong and very courageous, that you may observe to do according to all the law which Moses My servant commanded you; do not turn from it to the

---

[58] *TLOT*, 1:421.

right hand or to the left, that you may prosper wherever you go. This Book of the Law shall not depart from your mouth, but you shall meditate in it day and night, that you may observe to do according to all that is written in it. For then you will make your way prosperous, and then you will have good success. Have I not commanded you? Be strong and of good courage; do not be afraid, nor be dismayed, for the LORD your God *is* with you wherever you go (Josh. 1:2–9).

Ordination in the Old Testament

The concept of ordination in the Old Testament is intriguing.[59] There are a considerable number of Hebrew words that denote the idea of ordination. These words have fascinating meanings and nuances that bring richness to the concept of ordination. Both the Hebrew and Greek languages use several different words that can imply or may have been translated to mean "ordain." The Hebrew alone has about eleven different words implying ordination.[60]

> *'āmad*: stand, make to stand, appoint, establish (2 Chron. 11:15)

> *'ārak*: set in successive order, appoint (Ps. 132:17; Isa. 30:33)

> *'āśâh*: make, constitute, appoint (Num. 28:6; 1 Kings 12:32–33)

> *yāsad*: set, place, appoint, establish (1 Chron. 9:22; Ps. 8:2)

---

[59] This work is not addressing the current debate on women ordination. The material discussing women ordination is voluminous both in print and online. It is not necessary to review the literature or engage in the debate here. What frustrates many people in this discussion is the Bible's silence on ordaining women. However, this work explores the biblical concept of ordination and its relevance even in this time of the end.

[60] Wilson, *Old Testament Word Studies*, 296–297.

kûn: set upright, form, be fixed aright, settle, make permanent (Ps. 8:3)

m^enāh: number, constitute, appoint (Dan. 1:10; Dan. 2:24)

nātan: give (2 Kings 23:5; Jer. 1:5)

pā'al: work (emphatically), with attention, make ready (Ps. 7:13)

qûm: rise up, arise, stand (Esther 9:27)

śûm: set, put, place, establish, appoint, make a law (1 Chron. 17:9; Ps. 81:5; Hab. 1:12)

shāpaṭ: set, put, place in an even steady position (Isa. 26:12)

In the Hebrew language, the words that can be translated as *ordain* evince many shades of meanings that can be categorized mainly into four areas. Ordination is understood as:

(a) to put or arrange in order (Ps. 132:17; Isa. 30:33; Heb. 9:6),

(b) to establish or bring into existence (1 Kings 12:32; Num. 28:6; Ps. 8:2–3),

(c) to enact a decree (Esther 9:27; Acts 16:4; Rom. 7:10),

(d) to set apart, destine or appoint for an office or duty (Jer. 1:5; Mark 3:14; John 15:16; Acts 14:23; 1 Tim. 2:7; Titus 1:5; Heb. 5:1; Heb. 8:3).[61]

---

[61] *The New International Dictionary of the Bible*, eds. J. D. Douglas, Merrill C. Tenney (Grand Rapids: Zondervan, 1987), 737; D. Miall Edwards, "Ordain," in *The International Standard Bible Encyclopaedia*, eds. James Orr, et al. (Grand Rapids: Eerdmans, 1960), 4: 2199–2200; J. Hastings, "Ordain, Ordinance," *Dictionary of the Bible* (New York: Charles Scribner's Sons, 1903), 3: 631; W. White, "Ordain,"

Of the four nuances for ordination, the last one is popularized in our contemporary situation, but the meaning was never implied in the word. Ordination as we have come to understand it was practiced on priests, Levites, prophets, national leaders, and the messianic figure. Ordination is investing someone with ministerial or sacerdotal rank or power, and the setting apart of such an individual for an office in church ministry.

Another Hebrew word that is used with regard to ordination is *mālē'*, "to be full" or "to fill." It figuratively describes the ceremony of ordination. It was used in Numbers 3:3 and Exodus 29:9, where the sons of Aaron were ordained as priests. To ordain literally means to "fill their hand" (Exod. 28:41; Lev. 4:5; Lev. 8:33). The question that may linger in our minds is this: "What fills the hand of the person being ordained?" However, the filling of the hand of the person being ordained should not be limited to the provision of material blessings. Ordination is not a call to receiving stuff from God. The filling of the hand symbolically expressed the idea of empowerment to the office, as well as the assurance that the Lord would provide the qualifications necessary to function in that office.

It is noted that "this 'filling of the hand' signified two things in the ordination of priests. First, it represented the duty and the privilege the priest had in making offerings to the Lord on behalf of others. Second, it represented that the Lord would indeed fill their hand in the sense of providing for their material needs of the priests (KD 1:342). The ceremonial act of filling the hand represented God's sufficiency."[62] The Lord shall provide means for His work.

The Old Testament does not limit ordination to humans only. Some burnt offerings were ordained at Mount Sinai (Num. 28:6). Jeroboam ordained a feast in the eighth month (1 Kings 12:32–33). With regard to ordination, "an important theological truth is that the very presence or glory of the Lord fills certain things, places, or people."[63] We repeatedly see the awesome presence of God filling places as a stamp of His approval. The tabernacle of meeting was covered by a cloud and filled

---

The Zondervan Pictorial Encyclopedia of the Bible, ed. Merrill C. Tenney (Grand Rapids: Zondervan, 1976), 4: 542–543.

[62] *NIDOTTE*, 2: 940.

[63] *NIDOTTE*, 2: 940.

with the glory of God (Exod. 40:34–35). The temple of Solomon too had the cloud and the glory filling it up (1 Kings 8:10–11). The newly ordained Joshua was filled with the spirit of wisdom (Deut. 34:9).

Even in our day, it is evident that those whom God appoints for His purpose will be empowered.

> Those who consecrate body, soul, and spirit to God, will constantly receive a new endowment of physical, mental, and spiritual power. The inexhaustible supplies of heaven are at their command. Christ gives them the breath of His own Spirit, the life of His own life. The Holy Spirit puts forth His highest energies to work in heart and mind. The grace of God enlarges and multiplies their faculties, and every perfection of the divine nature comes to their assistance in the work of saving souls. Through co-operation with Christ, they are made complete in Him, and in their human weakness they are enabled to do the deeds of Omnipotence.[64]

The process of ordination in the Old Testament involved washing and clothing the priests in special garments made for their office. The high priest was anointed with olive oil poured on the head (Exod. 29; Lev. 8; Lev. 21:10). Several offerings and sacrifices were presented for the occasion (Exod. 29:1–35; Lev. 7:37; Lev. 8:14–36). The anointed priests were consecrated to serve the Lord among His people. In the Old Testament, ordination is the public investiture distinguishing the individual whom God had appointed for a specific role. It is the empowerment with authority and special abilities to execute the assigned task. Moses laid his hands on Joshua (Deut. 34:9). Laying hands effected the transfer of power and the Holy Spirit to fill the appointee for the designated office.

As can be noted in ancient Israel, they did not lay hands on one appointed to be a king.[65] Kings were anointed with oil on their heads

---

[64] Ellen G. White, *Gospel Workers* (Washington, DC: Review and Herald Publishing Association, 1915).

[65] Marjorie Warkentin, *Ordination: A Biblical-Historical View* (Grand Rapids: Eerdmans, 1982), 9–10.

before their enthronement (1 Sam. 9:16; 1 Sam. 10:1; 1 Sam. 15:1, 17; 1 Sam. 16:13; 1 Kings 1:39). Prophets anointed kings who were chosen by God and who were not in line of dynastic succession (1 Sam. 9:16; 1 Sam. 16:12; 2 Kings 9:1–6), but those kings who were appointed in line of dynastic succession were anointed by priests (1 Kings 1:39; 2 Kings 11:12). Priests seem to have been confined to anointing individual kings succeeding within the established order, whereas prophets were sent to individuals outside dynastic lines whom God invited to the throne.

Ordination in the New Testament

The New Testament practice of ordination reflects the Old Testament ceremony of laying hands. In the New Testament, "the word 'ordination' does not occur, and the verb 'to ordain' in the technical sense does not occur either."[66] Different versions of the New Testament translate several Greek verbs as *ordain,* but as shown in the list below, these verbs may only imply the concept. The idea of ordination does find expression through over twenty different Greek words that are descriptive of the ceremony. Each of these words has several nuances that enrich our understanding of what ordination is all about. Depending on the context, these words can be correctly translated as *ordain.* The concept of ordination is a relevant biblical practice. Similarly, the word *Trinity* does not appear in the Bible, but the concept of three coeternal divine persons is clear in the scripture. Some of the Greek words that express the concept of ordination include the following:

> *anadeíknumi:* mark out, appoint to a position or service (Luke 10:1; Acts 1:24)
>
> *anorthóō:* set straight up (Luke 13:13; Heb. 12:12)
>
> *apostéllō:* set apart, send forth (Mark 3:14; Luke 9:2; Acts 3:26; Acts 7:35)

---

[66] L. Morris, "Ordination," *The New Bible Dictionary,* ed. J. D. Douglas (Grand Rapids: Eerdmans, 1979), 912.

aphorízō: set off by boundary, exclude, separate (Matt. 13:49; Matt. 25:32; Acts 13:2)

gínomai: become, begin to be (Acts 1:22)

diatássō: arrange, charge, prescribe, appoint (1 Cor. 7:17; 1 Cor. 9:14; Gal. 3:19)

diachōrízō: apportion, separate (Luke 9:33)

eklégomai: choose, select (Luke 10:42; Titus 1:1)

entolē: command, charge, commission, order, ordinance (Rom. 7:10; 1 Tim. 6:13–14)

kathístēmi: set, place, constitute, put in a position (Titus 1:5; Heb. 5:1; Heb. 8:3)

kataskeuázō: prepare fully, put in readiness (Matt. 11:10; Mark 1:2; Luke 7:27; Heb. 9:6)

krínō: judge, separate, distinguish, select, determine (Acts 16:4)

poiéō: make, form, cause, produce (Mark 3:14)

prográphō: write before, proscribe, appoint (Rom. 15:4; Jude 4)

proetoimázō: prepare beforehand, predestinate, appoint before (Rom. 9:23; Eph. 2:10)

promeletáō: premeditate (Luke 21:14)

proorízō: determine or decree beforehand (Acts 4:28; Rom. 8:29–30; 1 Cor. 2:7) *protíthémi*: set before someone, propose, purpose, design beforehand (Rom. 1:13; Rom. 3:25)

tássō: place in order, appoint, arrange, set (Acts 13:48; Rom. 13:1)

títhēmi: set, put, place, lay (John 15:16; 1 Tim. 2:7)

cheirotonéō: stretching out the hands, constitute by voting (Acts 14:23; 2 Cor. 8:19)

horízō: mark by a limit, determine, appoint, constitute (Acts 10:42; Acts 17:31)

In the New Testament, the laying of hands on designated candidates becomes more prominent and defines what ordination is all about. However, the laying of hands on people is not always considered to be ordination in the sense of being appointed to a specific office. Hands are laid on children for a blessing (Matt. 19:13, 15) or on the sick for healing (Matt. 9:18; Mark 6:5; Mark 16:18; Luke 4:40; Luke 13:13; Acts 28:8). Believers receive the Holy Spirit at the laying of hands upon them (Acts 8:17).

The laying on of hands for different reasons is a continuation of the Old Testament practice. Hands were laid on children's heads for the conferring of a blessing, as seen in Genesis 48:8–22. Hands were also laid on the head of the sacrificed animal for symbolical transference of sin from the offender to the innocent animal (Lev. 4:4–33; Lev. 8:14, 18, 22; Lev. 16:21; Num. 8:12). The members of the religious community were told to lay their hands on a blasphemer's head before stoning the culprit to death (Lev. 24:14). The whole congregation of Israel laid their hands on the Levites when consecrating them for service (Num. 8:10). In distress, Tamar laid her own hand on her head (2 Sam. 13:19). The national leader, Joshua, was initiated into office through the laying on of hands. Figuratively, in both the Old and the New Testaments, laying a hand on someone, usually a condemned individual, implied attacking or killing that person (Exod. 7:4; 2 Kings 11:16; 2 Chron. 23:15; Neh. 13:21; Esther 2:21; Esther 3:6; Esther 6:2; Esther 8:7; Esther 9:2; Psalm 139:5;

Matt. 18:28; Matt. 26:50; Mark 14:46; John 7:30, 44; John 8:20; Acts 4:3; Acts 5:18; Acts 21:27). The occasion provided context that defined the reason for the laying of hands. Jesus laid His hand on John to strengthen him (Rev. 1:17).

Later development of the concept of ordination in the New Testament implied the laying of hands on certain individuals appointed for an office or mission. Matthias was chosen to take the place of Judas Iscariot, who had died. It is not clear whether Matthias was ever ordained. After having been chosen, he was simply "numbered with the eleven apostles" (Acts 1:26). The classical illustration of what ordination is all about is in Acts 6. Seven men were chosen to be deacons. Besides apostles, the office of the deacon was the first to be designated for the early Church. The office was created to fill the pertinent need that had developed while the Church was growing. The process of choosing the first deacons was simple. In the first place, there was the need for someone to serve. The twelve apostles summoned the entire congregation and gave them the qualifications of the men who were to be entrusted with the office of serving. The candidates had to be part of the congregation, men of good reputation, and also men filled with the Holy Spirit. Working together, the members of the congregation chose seven men and presented these before the apostles. The inauguration of these seven men was public. The apostles prayed and laid their hands on the newly chosen deacons. They began to serve with immediate effect, and the results were tremendous. God was glorified.

The appointment of the seven deacons established some precedents for the appointment of church leadership. The need for an officer arises in the congregation. This need is brought to the attention of the apostles, who in turn lay down the qualifications for the office bearer. The congregation is summoned to select the leadership they need. The apostles initiate the candidate through inauguration. Prayer and laying of hands on the appointee commissions and authorizes him to function in the designated office; there is no oil to be poured on the candidates here. Different words are used in the New Testament text that describe this occasion. It has come to be known as ordination.

The Holy Spirit initiated the appointment of Barnabas and Saul for missionary work (Acts 13:1–4). After much prayer and fasting, the prophets and teachers from the church at Antioch laid their hands on Barnabas and Saul and sent them away. The two men used this same procedure in the appointment of elders in every church they subsequently served. They fasted, prayed, and committed the newly appointed leaders to the Lord (Acts 14:23). Fasting and prayer preceded the laying of hands on the appointed leaders. Ordination was taken seriously because it meant dedication to God. This consecration demanded soul searching on the part of the appointees, on those who appointed, and on those who officiated. It was a form of sealing the fate of the candidates into the hands of God without reservation or option. When we eliminate fasting for those who are to be ordained, we miss a vital spiritual component in the preparation for the ordination ceremony.

As the early church grew and congregations were planted sporadically in distant places, there arose a need for leadership in each local venue. Paul instructed the believers regarding the procedures to be followed with regard to appointing leaders. The qualifications for an elder (1 Tim. 3:1–7; Titus 1:5–9) and for deacons (Acts 6:3; 1 Tim. 3:8–13) were clearly defined and became the standard for the Church. The laying of hands remains an important part of the Church's participation in joining with God in the calling and blessing of the person being ordained. This is to be done cautiously (1 Tim. 4:14; 1 Tim. 5:22; 2 Tim. 1:6).

Ordination in the End Times

In our religious world today, ordination means to appoint, certify, consecrate, dedicate, designate, destine, elevate, establish, inaugurate, induct, initiate, install, institute, invest, or set apart someone into a specific church or ministerial office, as well as the conferment of authority to function in that office. Our contemporary secular society views ordination merely as certifying or permitting someone to perform certain religious and social services. The ordained person may or may not have any religious affiliation at all. The public simply wants the services of an ordained person to function in some official capacity, including solemnizing marriages, conducting funerals, counseling, and chaplaincy. Many individuals who may be academically qualified seek ordination so that they may function in secular as well as religious capacities. Today, people can go online, read a few things on ordination, pay a little fee, and receive their ordination certificate. Now the individual seeks ordination so as to get a job somewhere, rather than waiting on God to designate a fit person to meet the need arising in the local religious community.

Ordination is installation of an individual into an ecclesiastical office. Obviously, ordination is a church thing. It is up to the Church organization to choose whom to ordain. The process of ordaining differs from place to place, but prominent are charging the candidates to perform their duties according to the guidelines laid out in God's word, and praying for their faithfulness. The ordained person can also execute public duties provided they do not conflict with one's religious ethic. We must be careful not to cheapen ordination by administering the ordinance as we see fit. We denigrate the concept of ordination if we use it simply to fulfill specific desires of the community of believers. Political, economic, sociocultural, or gender interests may have their place, but promotion of any one of these is not a reason for ordination. God is the one to decide who should be appointed for ordination. God's involvement in the life of the individual set for ordination must be evident. If the Church weakens its theology of ordination, this will bring in compromise with regard to other teachings as well.

Ordination is still a viable and much-needed church practice. As long as the church exists, and as long as the ministry demands workers, ordination will be necessary. There is no reason to believe that it should be abandoned in the time of the end. Distorted views on ordination have caused division in some church organizations. Individuals have differing perceptions with regard to the administering of this rite. Sadly, the ordination issue has become a battleground. Many are copying the people of ancient Israel during the time of the judges. At that time, each person did what was right in one's own eyes (Judg. 21:25).

Ordination is a God thing. God still wants to appoint His Spirit-filled leaders for the purpose of preparing believers for the soon coming of Jesus. We stand accountable for the abuse of this divine empowerment. Ordination must be done right, by the right officiants, upon the right candidates, and for the right reasons. Anything short of the biblical prescription for ordination is a disgrace!

Chapter 7

MATERIAL RESPONSE
TO GOD'S CALL

JUST BEFORE CROSSING over into Canaan, Moses reiterated the instructions on how to maintain the extensive system of offerings and sacrifices required of God's people once they settled in their new home. An offering can be a sacrifice, and a sacrifice can also be an offering. The two words are often used interchangeably in the biblical text. However, the primary meaning of the word *sacrifice* tends to be the animal that was killed and burned at the temple altar in a substitutionary role. The people were already accustomed to the sacrifices, offerings, and festivals because they had maintained these methods of worship since Mount Sinai. Specific offerings and sacrifices were appropriate for particular reasons. Offerings seem to stem from the ancient concept of maintaining the building and covering the operating expenses of the temple, which was regarded as the house of God. It was necessary to design ways and means to sustain the services at the temple. On the other hand, sacrifices had more to do with the maintaining or rebuilding of the divine-human relationship. The full-time personnel serving at the temple had to live on some of the offerings and sacrifices brought by the people.

While the people of Israel were travelling in the wilderness, they were asked to give resources for the construction and services of the tabernacle (Exod. 25:8). The people's response to this need was overwhelming. It is reported that people gave offerings in kind. Of interest is the fact that people gave from the willingness of their hearts (Exod. 35:21–29). The prerequisite for any giving, either back to God or to other humans, is the willingness of the heart. When people give freely, it is because they love to give. Love gives. It is interesting to note that ever since Moses called for freewill offerings, people continued to bring in stuff. Those who were receiving the offerings told Moses that there was too much stuff already. Moses had to restrain people from bringing in the offering (Exod. 36:5–7). If people are moved to give to the Lord, there will not be any lack of support for the advancement of God's purposes.

The Idea of Offering

The word *offering* is embedded with several concepts. It can refer to the act of making an offer, the presentation of a gift, the contribution made for religious purposes, or the object that is given. *Offering* is any material response that humans return to God in a designated setting for a specific purpose. It is giving in response to God's definite call. "The concept that the offering was in effect a gift from the offerer to God is also made explicit in the phrase … 'the gifts of the holy things' (Exod 28:38). Furthermore, the special feature of being 'set apart, made holy' is closely tied in with the view that the sacrifice is a gift."[67] We give what we own as a gift to someone. Sacrifice or offering is a personal expense to the giver. Araunah wanted to give King David his field, oxen, and wood for free so that the king would in turn build an altar for sacrificing to God. In his sanctified desire to make a personal offering to God, King David told Araunah that he would not give to the Lord something that did not cost him anything. King David decided to first buy the field and oxen from Araunah and then sacrificed burned offerings and fellowship offerings to God (2 Sam. 24:20–25). The giver must own what he or she gives (Num. 5:10).

The Bible does not really give us the origin of sacrifices and offerings. We simply come across the concept as we read the text. God must have illustrated the idea and instructed humans about the practice of sacrifices and offerings. The first time we learn about offering, it was the

---

[67] A. F. Rainey, "Sacrifice and Offerings," *The Zondervan Pictorial Encyclopedia of the Bible*, ed. Merril C. Tenney (Grand Rapids: Zondervan, 1976), 5:200.

wrong kind of offering, and God had rejected what was offered. Cain had brought an "offering of the fruit of the ground to the LORD" (Gen. 4:3). We read that God "did not respect Cain and his offering" (Gen. 4:5). Abel "brought of the firstborn of his flock and of their fat. And the LORD respected Abel and his offering" (Gen. 4:4). Clearly, God had instituted the idea of offering. The two boys were well instructed in the way how the sacrificial system works. However, they had to exercise their decisions independently on whether to follow God's prescription. Cain thought of improvising but that did not work for him. We see in Abel, an individual who took God for His word and followed instructions to fulfill the expectation of God. When we choose to obey God's word and do His will, God is glorified. What is disturbing is the fact that the first human being to die was Abel, who was murdered for giving the right offering to God (Gen. 4:8).

There are several different words used in the Old Testament to express more fully the concept of offering. Traditionally, the Hebrew 'iššeh depicts an offering, or at least that part of the offering that is consumed by fire on the altar.[68] Burnt offerings could be either an animal or a certain measure of grain (Lev. 2:1–3). This offering was consumed by fire in whole or in part. If it was partly burned, then the rest was given to the priest and the Levite and their families for their sustenance (Lev. 7:30–34). The burned offering was sometimes called holocaust offering (Greek: *holos* "whole," and *kaustos* "burned"). When this burned offering was done well and acceptable before God, it was depicted as "pleasing/soothing aroma" (Gen. 8:21; Eph. 5:2) to the Lord. Also 'iššeh was a generic term for all kinds of offerings including cereal/grain offerings (Lev. 2:3; Lev. 23:13), peace offerings (Lev. 3:3, 5, 9, 11, 14, 16; Lev. 7:25), guilt offerings (Lev. 7:5), and consecration offerings (Lev. 8:28).[69]

The significance of this kind of offering is that it could meet certain requirements for building the relationship between God and humans. The burned portion was expiatory as well as substitutionary in that the offerer would not face the consequences of his or her ill behavior before

---

[68] Mounce, *Mounce's Complete Expository Dictionary of the Old and New Testament Word*, 480.

[69] *TWOT*, 1:77; *NIDOTTE*, 1:542–543.

God. On the other hand, the consumed part was for fellowship and was also God's provision for the services rendered in the temple setting.

Other words that highlight the concept of offerings and sacrifices in Hebrew include "*qorbān* (that which is brought near, gift), *zebaḥ* (that which is slain, sacrifice), *minḥâh* (gift; also used more specifically for the cereal offering)."[70] The Greek has a rich vocabulary that broadens our understanding of sacrifices and offerings. The list includes "*prosphora* (offering), *dōron* (gift), *thysia* (sacrifice, also cereal offering) … *holokautōma* (whole burnt offering), *thymiama* (incense), [and] *spendō* (pour out as a drink offering)."[71]

Whatever was offered had to meet certain criteria. Specifically, there were animal sacrifices and also bloodless offerings. The animals accepted for sacrifices were of both sexes and were taken from among cattle, sheep, goats, and pigeons. The pigeons or turtle doves were mainly used by the poor, who could not afford the prescribed animals. When it comes to sacrifice, God directed that the poor and the wealthy can all afford to present something acceptable to the Lord. The animals offered were not to have any defect or blemish (Exod. 12:5; Lev. 22:18–25; Mal. 1:6–14). The bloodless offerings were either liquid or cash in kind. Whatever offering was specified by God was to be surrendered by the offerer in the correct way and with a cheerful attitude. Offerings or sacrifices could be communal or individual. In addition, individuals could participate in presenting offerings to the Lord on their own, as we see in the case of Cain, Abel, Noah, and many other individuals in the Bible. Later, when the office of the priest was established, the communal offerings were administered by the designated priests on behalf of all of the people.

For the most part, the book of Leviticus gives instructions about priests and Levites in their work of administering the sanctuary services. The first seven chapters of Leviticus outline the five main offerings—namely, burned (Lev. 1), grain (Lev. 2), fellowship (Lev. 3), sin (Lev. 4:1–5:13), and guilt (Lev. 5:14–6:7). There were also additional regulations for these offerings (Lev. 6:8–7:38). Sacrifices and offerings

---

[70] *New Dictionary of Biblical Theology*, ed. T. Desmond Alexander (Downers Grove, IL: InterVarsity Press, 2000), 754.

[71] Ibid.

were a major component of worship. While both sacrifices and offerings were required, offerings tended to be voluntary. Sacrifices were made from herds and flocks (Lev. 1:3–13). Birds were allowed as sacrifices for the poor people (Lev. 1:14–17; Lev. 5:7; Lev. 12:8; Luke 2:24).

When Israel had been settled in Canaan for a few hundred years, Solomon finished and dedicated a great temple to the Lord. We are informed that the Lord appeared by night after this event, at which time He talked to Solomon again. The Lord said, "I have heard your prayer, and have chosen this place for Myself as a house of sacrifice" (2 Chron. 7:12). The temple is thus designated "the house of sacrifice." This is the specific place to which people were to bring their sacrifices.

The motive for bringing either an offering or sacrifice is crucial. It can range from guilt to gratitude, from faith to adoration, but the overall purpose is to please God and secure His divine favor. Whatever a person does in relation to the temple, it has to do with sacrifice. Sacrifice implies surrendering what we possess to God. Worship is sacrifice, praise is sacrifice, singing is sacrifice, prayer is sacrifice, confession is sacrifice, and giving is sacrifice! Submitting ourselves to God's will is sacrifice (Rom. 12:1). Above all, sacrifice must be done right for it to be acceptable before God.

Catalogue of Offerings

While on the Plains of Moab, the Lord told to Moses to instruct Israel about the place of worship. Great importance was attached to the supporting of worship services at the central place that would be established for that purpose. Chapters 28 and 29 of Numbers illustrate what offerings were to be made, how, when, and where they were to be deposited. More on offerings is in Deuteronomy 14:22–29 and 26:1–19. Notice the fact that it is the Lord who brings the matter of offerings and sacrifices to Moses. It is very clear that offerings are a God thing. Those who bring the offerings and those who administer the offerings must first and foremost recognize that they are accountable to God.

Offerings and sacrifices were presented daily, weekly, monthly, and annually (Exod. 29:38–42; Lev. 23; Num. 28–29). In the Bible, the offerings and sacrifices had several specific purposes. First, people brought in offerings and sacrifices to support God's work at the temple. These could be used for various temple-related purposes, as specified in the text. They might be used at the place of worship for construction, maintenance, equipment, support of priests and Levites, or any other business of the Lord (see 2 Kings 12:4–5). The second reason for bringing in offerings and sacrifices was for the support of the poor and of the Levite. Part of this offering could be eaten at the designated place. They were required to share a portion of what they brought with the Levites and the poor. The third aspect of offerings was those designed for personal expiation and cleansing from moral defilement. When one had committed a sin, the offender would bring an animal that was going to be slain at the temple altar and burned as an expiation.

Sacrifices offered by Israel served three purposes.[72]

(1) As a gift, a sacrifice was meant for recognition, generosity, and gratitude towards the Lord God, who is the initial Giver of all that Israel possessed.
(2) The offering of an animal, in conjunction with vegetable sacrifices, created an occasion for joyous fellowship with each other over the resulting meal.
(3) Sacrifices provided the means for expiation of Israel's violation of the statutes of the Lord.

Israel gave a variety of offerings. A special offering could be levied on behalf of the Lord for a specific purpose. At the camp on the Plains of Moab, the Lord told Moses to collect a tribute from the men who went to war as a special offering to be handed over to Eleazar the Priest for the Lord (Num. 31:28–29). Another collection was taken up for the Levites who ran the sanctuary services (Num. 31:30). Passover, Pentecost, and the Feast of Tabernacles were some festivals that the children of Israel observed by divine command. The people were to bring their offerings when they traveled to these meetings. No one was to come empty-handed—that is, without a gift (Exod. 23:14–17; Exod. 34:18–23; Deut.

---

[72] Walter Brueggemann, *Worship in Ancient Israel: An Essential Guide* (Nashville: Abingdon, 2005), 20–21.

16:16–17). An important lesson for us is that we should always bring an offering when we come together for special occasions before our God. Ad hoc collections can be used to meet some special needs at God's house. In other words, it is an honor and privilege to finance God's business. Nehemiah 10:32–39 talks about giving gifts that would sustain God's work.

Offering Types

Sacrifices and offerings were surrendered for multiple reasons and purposes. Whether for personal or corporate delinquencies, sacrifices were given to show faith in God's remedy for sins committed by the people. Sacrifices were also presented to express the penitent's desire to be pure. Some sacrifices and offerings offered at the designated venue were brought as provision for food in God's house. This idea is clarified in Malachi 3:10, where God commands the people to bring all of the tithes, "that there may be food in My house." Thanksgiving and gratitude for God's providence prompted many to bring offerings and sacrifices to the Lord. People who realized that they were beneficiaries of God's goodness, blessing, or deliverance from either enemies or sickness responded extemporaneously by giving freewill offerings. Contributions were also made for specific projects in the community or at the center for worship.

The offerings that were meant to correct a person's moral standing before God illustrated the Lord's plan for reestablishing the relationship broken when sin brought separation between the individual or the group and God. When a person broke the covenant with the Lord, that person was required to suffer the consequences for the misbehavior. Any crime committed against God is sin. The penalty of sin is death (Gen. 2:17; Ezek. 18:4; Rom. 6:23). Iniquity is any crime against humanity. Iniquity committed against a fellow human being is also a sin against God. Yet God, through His grace, made provision for redeeming anyone who may have forfeited the claim to the covenant blessings. Instead of sentencing the offender to die, a substitute was to be brought and killed in place, thus atoning for the sinner and restoring the sinner to favor with God.

Most of the offerings brought to the Sanctuary, and later to the Temple, pointed forward to the real offering, Jesus Christ. The festivals likewise foreshadowed His plan of redemption for the people of the world. Paul points out that Jesus Christ has taken out of the way those things that were pointing to him (Col. 2:14). No longer should anyone judge us with regard to food, drink, festivals, or Sabbath days that were "a shadow of things to come" (Col. 2:16–17). Christ has already been nailed to the cross. Festivals, as well as offerings and sacrifices that were typical of Christ, ceased to have any value the moment Christ died on the cross. All things that pointed forward to the sacrificial death of Christ on the cross ended with His death.

The New Testament provides ample evidence that Christ was the sacrificial Lamb that was slain on our behalf (John 1:29). After the crucifixion of Christ on the cross, it is no longer necessary to kill lambs for our sins, or to bring food and drink offerings on certain days as prescribed in the Old Testament. That which pointed forward to Christ was replaced by Christ.

> The OT sacrifices provide providential categories for the interpretation of Christ's sacrifice, but it everywhere transcends those categories. For the blood of animals, we have the blood of the man Christ Jesus (Heb. 10:4). For spotlessness, we have sinlessness (Heb. 9:14; 1 Pet. 1:19). For a sweet smelling odor, we have true acceptability (Eph. 5:2). For the sprinkling of our bodies with blood, we have forgiveness (Heb. 9:13–14, 19–22; 1 Pet. 1:2). For symbolic atonement, endlessly repeated, we have real atonement, once for all (Heb. 10:1–10).[73]

When a sacrificial offering was laid on the altar to be burned, it was not to be retrieved. No regret or change of mind was permitted. God did not withdraw Christ from the cross. Once we offer ourselves as living sacrifices, we should not draw back. Any withdrawal from God is fatal to our spirituality. Sacrifice had immediate and future relevance. The immediate relevance had to do with the temporary cleansing of the one

---

[73] *New Dictionary of Biblical Theology*, 761.

who offered it. All sacrifices had implications for the future. They were practiced as evidence of faith in the once-and-for-all offering of the Lamb of God who takes away the sin of the world.

In summary, as ancient Israel prepared to cross over into Canaan, sacrifices and offerings would continue to be very important; these would maintain and sustain their extensive religious system. The priests and the Levites and their families were supported by portions of offerings and sacrifices brought by the people. The offerings and sacrifices were also vital in maintaining the people's relationship with their God.

> Under the Jewish economy, gifts and offerings formed an essential part of God's worship. The Israelites were taught to devote a tithe of all their income to the service of the sanctuary. Besides this they were to bring sin offerings, free-will gifts, and offering of gratitude. These were the means for supporting the ministry of the gospel for that time. God expects no less from us than He expected from His people anciently. The great work for the salvation of souls must be carried forward. In the tithe, with gifts and offerings, He has made provision for this work.[74]

Giving as Seen through the Eyes of Jesus

Jesus had a special interest in sacrifices and offerings. He explained the proper attitude in giving. Charitable giving is best done in secrecy (Matt. 6:1–4). The expression that one's left hand should not know what the right hand is doing in giving should not be taken literally. By using this figure of speech, Jesus is emphasizing the point that acceptable giving to the needy should not be a publicly advertised event. There is no room for blowing one's trumpet when presenting an offering. There is a reward that comes to those who have the right attitude in helping others. In Matthew 6, Jesus teaches about three virtues of piety–namely,

---

[74] Ellen G. White, *Christ Object Lessons* (Berrien Springs, MI: Andrews University Press, 2015), 320–321.

charitable giving (verses 1–4), prayer (verses 5–15), and fasting (verses 16–18). Each of these three virtues is best carried out secretly. Charitable giving comes first on this list.

Once Jesus outlined the three virtues of piety, He elaborated on the first one, charitable giving. Our hearts are being prepared for heaven, and so it makes sense for us to invest in heaven (Matt. 6:19–21; Luke 12:33–34). The state of the heart determines the real value of all giving. *Mammon* is an Aramaic word for wealth, possessions, or riches. Jesus personifies mammon and places it in juxtaposition with God. One must choose either God or mammon, but it is impossible to enthrone both in the same heart. Anxiety can ruin all our desire to give. Jesus warned us that undue concern over future needs can destroy our relationship with God and eliminate any desire for charitable giving (Matt. 6:25–34). Giving with gratitude is a means of demonstrating faith in God's provision for all of our future needs.

Jesus announced that loving a neighbor was more important than sacrifices and offerings (Mark 12:33). This was stated immediately after Jesus recited the laws of love in Deuteronomy 6:5 (Mark 12:30) and Leviticus 19:18 (Mark 12:31). Then Jesus sat near the place where people were bringing their offerings. He observed unnoticed while the well-to-do people came in style and pomp to present their ostentatious offerings. One poor widow came quietly, desiring no recognition from anyone. She surreptitiously placed her two coins into the receptacle. Those coins hardly amounted to anything, yet they were all she had. She emptied herself of all her pitiful wealth. This one offering, though smaller than any of the others, caught Jesus's attention. The Savior reads our hearts as we offer Him praise, offerings, and sacrifice. He told His disciples that the poor widow gave more than all who preceded her. She gave all that she had and left nothing at home (Mark 12:41–43; Luke 21:1–4). What a sacrifice! The little, given in faith and love for God, is greater than large gifts from careless hearts. In fact, "stewardship provides us a means to participate in God's activities, regardless how much or little we think we possess."[75] Jesus acknowledges even a cup of cold water given to someone who needs it (Matt. 10:42).

---

[75] Gary R. Councell, "Stewardship—A Two Way Street," *For God and Country* 3 (2016), 11.

The widow who brought two coins to the temple demonstrates much about sacrificial giving. The kind of giving that leaves you at a financial disadvantage is sacrificial giving. When your generosity leaves you at risk of being in want, this is sacrificial giving. Such giving is unusual in this world. Sacrificial giving is prompted by faith and acted upon through love. In sacrificial giving, "love is the atmosphere amid which faith should put forth its energy."[76] The sacrificial giver is aware of one's own limited resources, but the right combination of faith and love subordinates and eradicates personal and selfish desires.

Logic demands that individuals keep whatever they have for themselves, because the amount is not even enough for their immediate needs. However, the committed individual fully realizes God's call to give, and he or she decides by faith to respond to His bidding despite seemingly inadequate resources. Faith as a component in sacrificial giving is very important because we know that "without faith it is impossible to please God" (Heb. 11:6). By faith, we know that what little we have is from God, and faith surrenders that little back to God. This type of giving does not even expect God to compensate in any way. The person is concerned only about doing God's will. Sacrificial offering is giving above and beyond what is expected. It is indeed painful giving. Some encourage giving until it hurts. Sacrificial giving can lead you to make a commitment to give when you have nothing to give at the moment. A sacrificial spirit can, by faith, nurse that hope in you to give when God provides you with resources. God, who is the supreme provider, does not hesitate to acknowledge such a sacrifice.

Jesus was once the guest in the home of a Pharisee. He challenged the Pharisee by pointing out that Pharisees were more concerned with outward appearances rather than inward hygiene. He advised the Pharisee to give alms from the things he had (Luke 11:41). The pathway to a clean heart was to give alms from all that he owned. With Jesus, we know that acceptable giving before God must be prompted by a pure heart. It is not the amount that we give that is important; it is how we stand before God that counts. If we are corrupt, we cannot win God's approval no matter how generous our offerings appear. We should

---

[76] Frederic Rendall, "The Epistle to the Galatians," in *The Expositor's Greek Testament*, ed., W. Robertson Nicoll (Grand Rapids: Eerdmans, 1951), 3:184.

remember that Cain's offering was rejected because he was profane (Gen. 4:5–7).

Jesus talks about the great divide that becomes evident when He comes to redeem us. The distinction between the saved and the lost at the end will be just as clear as that of sheep and goats. The sheep represent those people who gave their resources to Jesus, and the goats are those who did not (Matt. 25:31–46). In this lesson, it seems that Jesus recognizes giving as having paved way for the salvation of His people. Of course, people do not give to be saved. They give because they appreciate the salvation they have received, and they give because it is the right thing to do. Sadly, those who have problems in giving to others may find themselves in a spiritual poverty that they cannot escape at the end of time.

Giving in the Early Church

The early church experienced exponential growth in the number of believers who eagerly looked forward to the return of Jesus. The need for community among these new believers resulted in having all things in common. This meant sharing everything they had (Acts 4:32–37). This communal ownership of everything had the potential to destroy all class distinctions and all discrimination. It could build up a strong family bond among all believers. This system works well as long as people remain pure in heart and are faithful to Christ's call upon their lives. In the early Church, one couple cheated in the sharing process and faced an untimely consequence (Acts 5:1–11). The Church had two funerals in one day. Unfaithfulness and dishonesty in sacrifices and offerings is a disaster. We should always remember that the Holy Spirit monitors all of our transactions and weighs all of our words. Sadly, the sharing of all things in common did not last long for the early Church. Some believers raised a genuine complaint that there was some favoritism going on among God's people (Acts 6:1). The Church attempted to fix the problem through bringing in conscientious leadership, but human selfishness infiltrated the hearts of some of the early believers and frustrated the sacrificial spirit.

The early Christian church then implemented an alternative plan for communal living. They introduced the collection of offerings to specifically support the underprivileged. Those who had more resources shared with those who were struggling to survive. When drought and famine hit certain areas, privileged believers elsewhere made collections and sent their gifts to the impoverished people (Acts 11:27–30). Paul became renowned for such collection of offerings (Gal. 2:10; 1 Cor. 16:1–4). Paul even remembered verbatim Jesus's counsel on giving. He recited the Lord's words to the Elders of Ephesus: "It is more blessed to give than to receive" (Acts 20:35). Paul gave sound counsel for generous giving (2 Cor. 9; Eph. 4:28). True believers support full time gospel workers from their means (Luke 10:7; 1 Cor. 9:7–15; 1 Tim. 5:18).

Some Giving Tips

Giving is our material response to God's call. We have so much for which to be grateful before the Lord. It is appropriate to develop the habit of giving to those who are in need with the same generosity we would wish them to have toward us were the circumstances reversed. It is also proper to give to the Lord as we come together for worship. We should remember that giving to the Lord should not only be limited to worship times. We can give to the Lord anytime and anywhere (Matt. 25:34–40). Ancient Israel was cautioned not to appear before the Lord empty-handed (Exod. 34:20; Deut. 16:16). We need to keep our ears open to God's call to be co-workers with Him in sacrificial giving. We need to give in such a way as to please God.

Sometimes we shrink back from giving because we may have the knowledge that the person will not use our gift to God's glory. We feel that we want to be responsible stewards of the finances God has entrusted to us. We must be careful about this train of thought. If we refrain from giving to people in need because we think the recipients might not spend the money as we would, it could leave us in the same position as those unfortunate ones who came at the end of time and said to Jesus, "Lord, when did we see You hungry or thirsty or a stranger or naked or sick or in prison, and did not minister to You?" (Matt.

25:44). In our communities, we should be known for a practical love that alleviates the hardships of those who are going through difficult times. Giving food, clothes, shelter, and any other necessary form of assistance to those in need paves the way for those people to appreciate the character of Jesus.

When God called for offerings to build the tabernacle and establish its services, He pointed out the primary requirement to giving. Offerings as well as sacrifices that we give to God must be given with a willing heart in order to be acceptable (Exod. 25:2). This rule also applies in giving to individuals. Humans are good detectors of hypocrisy in those who give to them grudgingly. Needs may be supplied, but the lack of love may spoil the gift. Willingness is the antidote to all selfishness. Willingness to give is prompted by love. Love detects the real needs of others and is eager to give (John 3:16). Giving becomes most enjoyable and effective if it is planned giving. A good personal budget makes provision for giving. A truly generous giver is a cheerful giver. Generous giving is not only limited to giving plenteously of our finances. It also has to do with giving cheerfully and freely of ourselves. Giving grudgingly is condemned (Deut. 15:10; Gal. 6:7). The purity of our hearts in giving to meet the needs of others is the measure of our religion (James 1:27).

Anybody can bring to the Church tithe, offerings, gifts, thankful offerings, freewill offerings, and the like. This must be done with the full knowledge that by bringing in the tithe of our income, we are not giving anything to God. Tithe already belongs to God (Lev. 27:30; Mal. 3:8–11). We never own the tithe. God hands tithe in trust to us, and so we return that tithe back to God where it belongs. In this transaction He requires that we be found faithful custodians (1 Cor. 4:2). Our giving begins *after* we return the tithe back to God. Whatever we give after that reflects what is in our hearts.

The image of sowing and reaping is pertinent to our giving. The Old Testament illustrates good giving as scattering the seed generously, leading to abundant blessedness (Prov. 11:24–25). This idea is elaborated upon by Paul.

> But this *I say:* He who sows sparingly will also reap sparingly, and he who sows bountifully will also reap

bountifully. *So let* each one *give* as he purposes in his heart, not grudgingly or of necessity; for God loves a cheerful giver. And God *is* able to make all grace abound toward you, that you, always having all sufficiency in all *things,* may have an abundance for every good work. As it is written: "He has dispersed abroad, He has given to the poor; His righteousness endures forever." Now may He who supplies seed to the sower, and bread for food, supply and multiply the seed you have *sown* and increase the fruits of your righteousness, while *you are* enriched in everything for all liberality, which causes thanksgiving through us to God (2 Cor. 9:6–11).

Giving cures selfishness. If you give, you will be given more in return (Luke 6:38; Rom. 12:8). Jesus cautioned the religious leaders of the day that they tithed in great detail but neglected the most important things about God (Matt. 23:23; Luke 11:42). In other words, Jesus pointed out that along with tithing, they needed also to engage in justice, mercy, and faith in their daily lives. Complete obedience to God in everything is the prerequisite to success in anything we do in the name of God (see Jer. 7:21–23; Hosea 6:6; Amos 5:21–27; Mic. 6:6–8; 1 Pet. 1:2).

Giving in the Last Days

The demand for offerings is getting out of hand in this age of social media and ubiquitous advertising. Anybody can tell a sad story and collect offerings from people who think it sounds like a good cause. Some people spend their lives soliciting donations from generous people for their own personal gain. Taking advantage of people's generosity is a booming industry. Most of the money solicited evades the tax collectors. People are manipulated to give through some devious means. "Give, and you will be blessed by God!" is the appeal that drives many to be generous. Many such promotions are backed up by some biblical passages taken out of context. Every individual must carefully study the Bible. Each must be guarded by prayer and grounded in its truth to safeguard generosity and ensure that gifts and offerings are given to projects approved by God.

The systematic and benevolent giving of offerings was very important for Israel as they prepared to go into Canaan. These offerings were to sustain the extensive religious system established by God through Moses. For those of us who live at the very end of this world's history, offerings are even more important. As long as the gospel commission is not yet done (Matt. 28:19–20; Rev. 14:6–12), sacrificial offerings will continue to sustain God's divine work of saving souls who will go over with us into the Promised Land. If our hearts are right, our insufficiency in giving will not keep Jesus from coming back. God has promised to cut short His work in righteousness (Rom. 9:28). One day soon, people will want to give for the advancement of God's work, but they will not be able to do so because the work will already be done. Let us not be among those who become generous too late! Bless the Lord, O my soul!

Chapter 8

VENGEANCE ON ENEMIES

IN A BIBLE class, one of the new believers asked the teacher a question. He wanted to know what the teacher would do should he see a person killing another person. The unscrupulous teacher told the class that if it were him, he would kill the perpetrator. I had to respond quickly to this theological misconception by asking the audience to have a fresh look at that scenario. First, I pointed the class to Exodus 20:13, which unequivocally prohibits murder. Second, I raised the conscientious bar by referring to Matthew 5:21–22, where Jesus even condemns anger against someone. I commented that it was not appropriate for anyone, at any moment, to take the law into his or her own hands. The best the person who witnesses a murder can do is to report it to the responsible authorities as quickly as possible. I concluded by saying that as individuals, we needed to lead a prayerful life, including asking God daily for wisdom to function for His glory should we be caught up in unusual situations.

The idea of returning an injury for an injury is ingrained in many people's minds. This is the human cry for justice, and it is based upon and illustrated in the biblical text (Num. 35:16–24). It has not been a perfect solution because many people in the Bible went on with their lives without receiving deserved punishment for their offences. We generally feel insecure in the presence of someone who is opposed to us. This tends to cause a fight-or-flight reaction in us. However, enmity appears early in the Bible as a remedy to secure the relationship between humans and God. Enmity is a God thing. God placed enmity between humans and Satan as an instrument to keep these contending parties apart (Gen. 3:15). Enmity is appropriate as long as it serves its divinely designated purpose—that is, to safeguard humans from giving loyalty to the devil, the enemy of God. The enemy will finally be crushed. The biblical text states that whoever is an enemy to God's people, is also an enemy to God (Exod. 23:22; Num. 10:9; Num. 14:42; Num. 32:21). God will stand and protect His own. The warning was clear that whoever touches God's people touches the apple of God's eye (Zech. 2:8).

At the last camp before crossing the Jordan, provision was made for anyone who accidentally caused the demise of another. The perpetrator was supposed to run immediately, and as fast as possible, to one of the designated cities of refuge and find shelter there. Six such centers were to be scattered in the country. The Bible talks about these cities of refuge in Exodus 21:13, Numbers 35:6, 9–34, Deuteronomy 19, and Joshua 20. The legal system in place at the time would review and address the case of the manslayer. The guilty would face the rule of the law while the innocent would be restored into the community. The idea was to maintain sanity in the community (Deut. 19:20). When violence and wickedness characterize people in our communities, it is most likely to affect justice in the legal system in different ways. We are living in times when the legal systems in the nations of the world are easily manipulated. Powerful and rich people easily escape the consequences of their own atrocities while the disadvantaged poor are thrown into despair to struggle with the tyranny of injustice.

The Rise of Midianites

The Midianites were descendants of Abraham. After the death of Sarah, Abraham married Keturah. The fourth son of Abraham and Keturah was Midian, who became the eponymous ancestor of the South Transjordan people, known as the Midianites. The Midianites are sometimes known also as Ishmaelites (Gen. 37:25, 28, 36). Abraham sent all of his sons to live in distant desert lands away from Isaac (Gen. 25:6). They became ancestors of different tribes of the people collectively known today as Arabs. The interaction between the descendants of

Isaac and the descendents of the other sons of Abraham figures largely in Israelite history.

Joseph was sold by his brothers to the Midianite or Ishmaelite traders who took him down to Egypt and sold him there. The whole family later moved down into Egypt. After a while, Moses escaped justice when he fled from the pharaoh and dwelt in the land of Midian with the priest there. He married Zipporah, one of the seven daughters of the priest Jethro (Exod. 3:1; Exod. 4:18; Exod. 18:1). This Jethro was also known as Reuel (Exod. 2:18) the Kenite (Judg. 1:16). This same Jethro came to visit with Moses when Israel was camping at Mount Sinai. Moses and all the people gained much wisdom from Jethro's insight into administrative strategies (Exod. 18). Moses invited Hobab, Jethro's son, to accompany Israel to Canaan (Num. 10:29–32). Moses expected to benefit from Hobab's experience in desert travels. Later, we read of Jael, the wife of Heber the Kenite, slaying Sisera, the commander of an enemy army (Judg. 4:17–23; Judg. 5:24). Though not a Hebrew, Jael brought great deliverance to Israel. God can use anyone who is willing to bring deliverance to God's people in times of distress.

The Midianites continued to be a menace to Israel for a long time after Israel had settled in Canaan. We read of marauding bands of Midianite looters (Judg. 6–8). These Midianite thieves played havoc with Israel's economic resources, stealing whatever they wanted and destroying what they could not carry away. They were bitter enemies of Israel. The crimes they committed against God's people were committed against God in a way. When the time was right, God took vengeance against these people because of their wickedness.

Moses's Last Battle

Israel faced resistance from the joint forces of Moab and Midian when they were about to go in and take Canaan. This conflict resulted in the hiring of a prophet, Balaam, who was renowned for his success at casting spells, whether for blessing or for cursing. Balaam's attempt to curse Israel was a great failure in the eyes of those who hated God's people. However, Balaam found another way. He advised Israel's enemies to entice Israel through their wanton women. As a result, the men of Israel participated in harlotry with the women at Baal of Peor (Num. 25:3–18). God wiped out all of the culprits who were involved with the heathen women. Sadly, twenty-four thousand people were lost in this disaster. This incident heightened the tension between Israel and these neighboring nations.

Israel faced some serious sociopolitical struggles just before they crossed into the land of promise. Similarly, during the time of the end, those who are serious about going to heaven will face some challenges due to their faith commitment. When tempted with the allurements of the world, many will compromise their faith and fail to get to heaven.

Moses was winding up his leadership tenure when God instructed him to wage his final battle. Sometimes we think that we have finished our work, but if God still has some unfinished business, we dare not seek to escape. Many retirees keep on serving; God knows when we are done. After the incident with Cozbi and Zimri, God had told Moses to "harass the Midianites, and attack them" (Num. 25:16–18). To harass is to show hostility against, to vex or to treat with enmity.[77] The Midianites were deserving of such treatment not only because of their unkindness toward Israel, but also because they seduced Israel into harlotry. Once again we see that God took responsibility for dealing with the Midianites regarding their crimes against His people.

Numbers 31 begins with God instructing Moses to take vengeance on the Midianites for the distress they caused to the children of Israel. This was God's final task for Moses before his death. Moses did not hesitate to do what he was told to do, even though he knew that his death would follow the completion of that task. The old leader recruited fighters and organized them for war. The select army for Israel was drawn from all tribes except the Levites (Num. 1:4–50; Num. 26:57–62). Phineas, who had earlier distinguished himself by destroying the rebellious man of Israel along with his Midianite girlfriend, was assigned to act as the spiritual leader of the army during the conflict. In our contemporary society, we have chaplains who accompany the army when they go for war. Chaplains are non-combatants who provide

---

[77] *BDB*, 865.

spiritual and emotional support to the soldiers who are required to take on important national assignments.

Israel's army defeated and devastated the Midianites. Nevertheless, the army did not do exactly as God had told them to do. They failed to kill all of the males. They kept the small boys alive and brought them to the Israelite camp, along with the women. Triumphantly, the army arrived back at the camp of Israel and paraded all of the captives, animals, and goods. But when Moses came out to meet the returnees from war, he condemned the army officers for sparing the boys and for bringing to Israel the women who had caused thousands in Israel to die by the plague. Why the army officials (and even Phineas) failed to follow the instructions, and why they ended up bringing the women to Israel, is a puzzle. We would naturally expect Phineas to have objected to the idea of bringing Midianite women back into the camp, but no objection is recorded. Phineas represents some religious leaders who are not consistent in their zeal for the Lord. Such leaders stand up strong against certain issues but disregard other important matters. We often wonder at such inconsistency. God is glorified by leaders who are sensitive to the leading of the Holy Spirit and who rely on God's word all of the time.

Spiritual leaders face many issues that need to be seriously considered. Whenever we are on God's errands, it is imperative to abide by the instructions given, down to the minutest detail. When God takes the trouble to say something, it matters. We cannot rationalize away any part of God's word. We cannot have it our own way. We cannot ignore any moral safeguards. What God says is said for a reason, whether or not we understand what that reason is. We should be very conscientious about God's word in our time. Moreover, we should be careful not to add to what God says, or subtract anything from His words (Deut. 4:2; Prov. 30:6; Rev. 22:18–19). Later in Israelite history, the prophet Samuel rebuked King Saul for failure to follow God's instructions carefully: "Has the LORD *as great* delight in burnt offerings and sacrifices, as in obeying the voice of the LORD? Behold, to obey is better than sacrifice, *and* to heed than the fat of rams" (1 Sam. 15:22).

Biblical Concept of Vengeance

Just before Israel was to go into the land of promise, Moses was instructed by God to pay back the Midianites for the evil they did to God's people (Num. 25:16–18). As mentioned earlier, this was the last time God would send Moses into battle. Moses could not go across into the land of Canaan because of his own mistake in failing to follow God's command to the letter. Moses learned his lesson. Before his death, he carefully instructed Joshua, and the whole nation crossing over into Canaan, to be sure to observe whatever the Lord had taught them on the way.

We see that God instructed Moses to punish the Midianites for the harassment they had inflicted on Israel (Num. 31). This incident leads many to question the Bible. Some people see this as God demonstrating a vindictive attitude. The fact that it was God who ordered this genocide has led many readers to condemn the scriptures for fostering a revengeful spirit among those who follow God. Moreover, the Bible has several other examples where vengeance is carried out on the enemies of God's people. The song of Moses says, "vengeance is mine, and recompense" (Deut. 32:35; Rom. 12:19; Heb. 10:30). Vengeance was called for against certain of Israel's enemies, yet God told Israel that they were not to avenge themselves or bear grudges against each other (Lev. 19:18). The Psalmist reminds us that vengeance belongs to the Lord God (Ps. 94:1). The original meaning of the biblical concept of vengeance pointed to punishment that rectifies and cancels an injustice.[78]

Usually, vengeance was administered to people who were outside the confines of one's ethnic group; Moses illustrated this in Egypt (Exod. 2:11–15). If an atrocity was committed within the same ethnic group, then vengeance was not something individuals were allowed to do on their own (Lev. 19:18). The legal system was to catch up with the offender and inflict corresponding retribution, up to and including capital punishment. Vengeance was inflicted on the enemy, whether an individual or the entire nation. It is important to note that vengeance was always a divine directive. Humans could only administer vengeance when commissioned to do so by God. God has the right to command

---

[78] *TLOT*, 2:768.

vengeance, because God is the final arbiter of human behavior. God is the highest authority who settles all disputes.

The individual who has been wronged wants the perpetrator to be punished. If the offended died, then the related survivors looked forward to avenging the death of their relative. Some biblical Psalms seem to demand retribution or misfortune on enemies. Such passages are known as imprecatory Psalms; examples are Psalms 7, 35, 55, 58, 59, 69, 79, 83 109, 137, and 139. To imprecate means to call upon God's wrath to be poured down upon evil people. In these imprecatory Psalms, we see prayers for God to afflict or destroy the enemy for the wrong they have caused. The Psalms seems to sound very unethical to us in the way they address personal problems. Should a Christian call for evil upon one's enemies? Do imprecations militate against the teachings of Jesus in the New Testament? Interestingly, we see some imprecations, even in the New Testament (Acts 1:20; Acts 13:10–11; Rom. 11:9–10; 2 Tim. 4:14). There is also a pertinent cry for vengeance in Revelation 6:10.

The followers of Jesus are called to love their enemies and bless those who curse them (Matt. 5:44). Retaliating is absolutely forbidden (Matt. 5:38–42). Jesus rebuked His disciples strongly for seeking vengeance against the Samaritans who had failed to offer them hospitality (Luke 9:54–56). A Christian must not even think vengeful thoughts about another person (Matt. 5:21–26). It is interesting to notice that the New Testament's teaching on how to treat our enemies has not radically departed from the Old Testament teaching. The law of loving our enemies is an Old Testament motif (Exod. 23:4–5; Lev. 19:18; Deut. 23:7; Prov. 24:17). Paying evil for evil is forbidden in Proverbs 20:22. When it comes to dealing with our enemies, the Bible has been consistent in both Old and New Testament times. God's people appeal to God for His intervention on their behalf to destroy their enemies. God may use His faithful people or anyone else to execute vengeance on His behalf, but God alone is responsible for that.

There seems to be some tension between the negative demands for revenge on our enemies and the call for loving them. It is clear that vengeance belongs to God and God alone. God chooses those whom He wants to use in executing revenge. As humans, we call to God to intervene and God does effect vengeance when He sees it to be appropriate. The imprecations in the Bible are an appeal to God for Him to intervene and exterminate evil. Dr. Joel Musvosvi expressed it well: "the question of divine vengeance has to do with the implications of covenant lordship in a moral universe, not with the human desire for revenge and retaliation for injury suffered."[79] It is God who orders vengeance and is responsible for its execution.

Extermination of Amalek

Esau's firstborn son, Eliphaz, fathered a son, Amalek, through a concubine named Timna (Gen. 36:11–12). This Amalek is said to be the eponymous father of the Amalekites (Gen. 36:15–16). This being the case, we have to explain the Amalekites who appeared in Genesis 14:7 before Abraham had a son. Scholars have considered the appearance of the name Amalekites in Genesis 14:7 as "an anachronism which must be explained as an editorial insertion."[80]

However, the Amalekites seemed to have been loosely connected nomadic people spreading mostly through the southern part of Canaan (Exod. 17:8–16; Num. 13:29; Num. 14:25, 43, 45; Judg. 3:13; Judg. 5:14; 1 Sam. 15:2–32; 2 Sam. 1:1, 8, 13).

Another genocide is ordered by God in Deuteronomy 25:17–19. This time it is the people of Amalek who are to be wiped out. Their crime is clearly stated; the verdict is final. We know that Amalek came from behind Israel and attacked them when they were tired and weary. Another charge laid against Amalek is that they did not fear God at all. In Exodus 17:8–16, when Israel was at Rephidim, Amalek came over and fought Israel. This was the battle where Joshua proved his worth as God's appointed leader of the armies of Israel. Amalek was defeated, and this battle was recorded in the chronicles of Israel. Despite Israel's victory over Amalek at Rephidim, some of the Amalekites escaped. God commanded those Israelites who went over into Canaan to remember that it was their duty to blot out Amalek from earth.

Balaam prophesied about the extinction of the ancient nation of

---

[79] Joel Nobel Musvosvi, *Vengeance in the Apocalypse* (Berrien Springs, MI: Andrews University Press, 1993), 143.

[80] Gerald L. Mattingly, "Amalek," *Eerdmans Dictionary of the Bible* (2000), 48.

Amalek (Num. 24:20, 24). In Deuteronomy 25:17–19, God reminds Israel of the annihilation of the Amalekites when Israel is finally settled in Canaan. When Balaam made his prophecy concerning Amalek, he was not being creative in any way. It was already public knowledge that God had given a directive regarding the utter destruction of the Amalekites in Exodus 17:14–16. There is a lesson here for us who live during the time of the end. We must be careful not to be deceived by the devil. He may appear as an angel of light, but his intention is to deceive many (2 Cor. 11:13–15). False prophets and false teachers are among us. When they predict something that comes to pass, it does not mean that they are connected with God. No, a true prophet of God subscribes to all of the teachings of God. Also, the life of God's prophet must be in accordance with the demands of God's righteousness. Miracles alone are not a commanding determinant of the presence of God in anyone's life.

Crying Out to God

The picture depicted in Revelation 6:9–10 is disturbing. The souls of those who had been ruthlessly killed for the word of God cry out. They ask a question: "How long, O Lord, holy and true, until You judge and avenge our blood on those who dwell on earth?" (Rev. 6:10). The imagery we see in this passage can be understood more clearly from its Old Testament perspective. In the sanctuary service, the blood drained from the sacrificial animal was poured beneath the altar (Lev. 4:7; Lev. 8:15; Lev. 9:9). Blood is life (Lev. 17:11–14). The blood of Abel is said to be crying from the ground where it was poured out by Cain (Gen. 4:10).

Abel was martyred because of his faithfulness to the word of God. The souls in Revelation 6:9–10 were martyred because they were faithful to the word of God. Both the blood of Abel and the blood spilled under the altar by later martyrs cry to God for righteous retribution. The cries to God here must be understood "as appeals made by loyal subjects to their faithful Lord to vindicate them."[81]

More important, these cries to God from the souls are "a legal plea for the heavenly Judge, who is Holy and True, to retry their cases and to

---

[81] Musvosvi, *Vengeance in the Apocalypse*, 276.

render a verdict that will vindicate them and demonstrate the integrity of God as Lord and Protector of the covenant community that has unjustly suffered."[82] The message portrayed here comforts all who suffer and lose their lives for the sake of their faithfulness to God. It gives hope to all that God Himself will, at the end, vindicate His covenant-keeping people and finally put an end to the enemy.

---

[82] Ibid., 278.

Chapter 9

TWO AND A HALF PEOPLE

MANY AMAZING THINGS took place at the camp on the Plains of Moab. The elite army of ancient Israel went out, engaged in a battle with the Midianites, and defeated them. As victors, the army brought back captives to the camp near the Jordan. This is reminiscent of ancient Near Eastern kings who always brought back to their country some captives and war booty as a symbol of their success. Many reliefs discovered by archaeologists in the vast area of the Middle East show kings leading captives back to their homes after a victorious conquest.

Israel brought livestock and all kinds of goods into the camp as war plunder (Num. 31:9). Among the things looted was plenty of gold, silver, bronze, iron, tin, and lead (Num. 31:22). The Lord instructed Moses, along with Eleazar the priest and other community leaders, to take careful inventory of the plunder. This was to be divided into two equal parts. One part was for the men who participated in the war. The rest was shared among the community members who remained in the camp. The sharing of the plunder was well received by the people who had not worked for this. The idea of receiving free stuff thrills the hearts of people everywhere, even to date.

At the outset of their journey from Egypt, Moses had instructed Israel to ask the Egyptians for articles of silver and gold, and for clothing (Exod. 12:35–36). This fundraising effort was met with overwhelming success. The Egyptians, who had gone through ten horrendous national disasters, gave liberally when asked to do so by the Israelites. At the end of their forty years of wilderness travel, Israel is seen again appropriating free stuff. This time, they collected booty from a defeated enemy. This was another reaping of the benefits for their hard life of travel. We notice that just before crossing into the land of promise, God prepared the way for Israel to start building up their resources to make life easier when they arrived at their new home. God is gracious in many ways to His people. He provides what we need at the right time, sometimes at the expense of someone else.

Before crossing the Jordan River, while Israel was still camped on the Plains of Moab, they had several other battles with nations that militated against them. Israel was victorious over each of these nations, and their territory was left unoccupied because many of their people were killed in the battle. The original intention for fighting with these nations before crossing the Jordan was not for occupancy. Israel was simply dealing with the enemies who sought to prevent them from entering into the land of promise. Israel's success in battle was God's method of taking vengeance on some of these people for the atrocities they had committed against Him (Num. 31:1–3).

Enticed by Geography

After assessing the geographical features of the land east of the Jordan River, the tribes of Reuben and Gad discovered that this grassy landscape was excellent for raising livestock. The area was vast, and nobody was currently claiming this land. They liked the land. Already, they had lots of animals, which they had acquired as war booty. The two tribes decided to apply for permission not to cross the River Jordan with the rest of the tribes (Num. 32:1–5). They wanted to settle in this area east of the Jordan and receive it for their inheritance. The leaders of the tribes of Reuben and Gad brought their request to the leaders of Israel. They were looking for official consent to establish themselves on the opposite side of the Jordan from the land of promise. This is what many people do. When they have decided on what they want, they seek for endorsement from the authorities. Such acknowledgment offers them some sense of security and peace of mind. It also offers feelings ranging from achievement to contentment to know that their wish is officially approved. In this particular case, it was vital to find out whether God approved their plan.

Moses, Eleazar, and the community leaders were shocked to learn of the request by the tribes of Reuben and Gad (Num. 32:6–15). It sounded like some of the tribes were beginning to draw back from supporting the mission to conquer Canaan. Moses feared that what these two tribes desired would dishearten the other tribes who were bound to go and possess the land that God had promised them. Their request seemed to have the potential to damage the tribal fraternity of the nation. Moses objected to their petition because he feared a diminished commitment to the corporate plan for occupying the land across the Jordan. All tribes must rally together to overcome the dwellers of the new homeland. Israel was in the last stages of their forty-year expedition. To have some people falter here was disconcerting. Moses cited a similar incident that had occurred earlier at Kadesh Barnea (Num. 32:8). The people who discouraged others at Kadesh Barnea incurred the Lord's anger. Because of that insurrection, the culprits were not allowed to have the privilege and honor of making it into Canaan. All of those who were twenty years old and above died in the wilderness as punishment for their treason. They did not reach the anticipated destination because of their bad choices.

The request made by these two tribes soon became common knowledge among the other tribes of Israel. There were some sympathizers. The people watched to see the outcome of the negotiations between the two tribes and Moses, along with other community leaders. At this time, half the tribe of Manasseh was also convinced that they wanted to stay on the east side of the Jordan (Num. 32:33). There, they saw enough grasslands for their animals and promising lands for their settlement. The split in the tribe of Manasseh is significant. It is about family. Half of this tribe decided to part company with the rest. They chose to stay on the other side of the river. We know that the tribe of Manasseh originated from Joseph.

When Jacob was on his deathbed, Joseph brought his two sons for blessings as the custom of the day demanded (Gen. 48). Manasseh was Joseph's firstborn and should have had the primary portion of the blessings. Instead, Jacob gave Ephraim, the younger son, the birthright blessing despite Joseph's protests (Gen. 48:17–19). Of significance here are Grandfather Jacob's words in blessing Manasseh: "truly his younger brother shall be greater than he" (Gen. 48:19). The prominence of younger brothers over their older brothers is not unique here.[83]

It was from the tribe of Ephraim, Joseph's younger son, that God appointed a man to lead Israel back into Canaan. When it comes to crossing the Jordan River and settling into Canaan, half the tribe of Manasseh were content to stay outside the borders of the collective homeland. They had reached their own Canaan. Interestingly, the people of Manasseh who received permission to remain on the east side of the Jordan later went to fight for some land to occupy in Gilead (Num. 32:39–42).

It has become more and more commonplace to see members of our families giving up on family goals and choosing to be on their own. They may feel that they have good reasons and that their choices are going to improve their lives. Often those family members who disconnect themselves from the group in order to pursue financial gain also end up distancing themselves from God's counsel. In these last days on earth, we need to be very careful to safeguard and protect our church families from that which can distract us from the straight and narrow way to heaven. It is easy to be like Demas, who absconded from his faith journey and chose the worldly life offered at Thessalonica (2 Tim. 4:10). Each individual in every family has to make a personal choice about whether or not to go to heaven. The last days will be very trying times. Many individual church members have been lost as they draw back into the world. In some cases, whole church groups have strayed from God's counsel. People give up their faith despite the fact that the coming of Jesus is so near. It has also been noted that people who give up at the last minute can discourage others who would want to remain faithful to the high calling of God (Num. 32:7, 9). The absconders can derail the entire mission of a family or church. However, those who remain faithful to

---

[83] The motif of younger sons becoming more preferred than the older ones dominates many biblical passages. In Genesis, Seth was over Cain, Shem was over Japheth, Isaac was over Ishmael, Jacob was over Esau, and Judah and Joseph were over their brothers. Now, Ephraim was over Manasseh. See also 1 Chron. 5:1—2, and 1 Chron. 26:10.

their God and committed to His goals will achieve the desire of their hearts. It is easy to understand why Moses at first had a very negative view of the request of the tribes of Reuben, Gad, and the half-tribe of Manasseh.

Back in Egypt, the pharaoh had asked Moses and Aaron a question about who would actually go with them on their pilgrimage to worship God (Exod. 10:8). In reply, Moses told the pharaoh that the expedition would not leave anyone behind. The young, the old, and sons and daughters would go. They would even take all of their animals with them. As Israel left Egypt together, I am sure that they had hoped to enter Canaan together. But many perished along the way because of their own stubbornness and wickedness. Now, at the final stage of their journey, two and a half tribes chose not to cross over into Canaan. They were eligible to cross over the Jordan but decided at the last minute not to do so. They wanted to remain on this side of the river because they got what they wanted already. It is true that every person is eligible to go to heaven through Christ's offer, but many will not make that choice.

Of all the people who came out of Egypt with the plan to go to Canaan, there existed two distinct groups of people who would not settle in Canaan. Those who died on the way because of their wickedness were found in the first group. The other group was made up of those who survived to the border but made a personal choice not to cross over and settle in Canaan. At the end of time, we know that the wicked dead will not be able to go to heaven. The living wicked—those alive at the coming of Jesus—will not make it into heaven because they have already decided to claim the treasures they have found on this side of heaven.

We must always be cautious of people who drop out from important group activities such as church attendance in these last days. They may have reasonable-sounding reasons for doing so, but a few individuals who abscond from the mission of the Church, whether suddenly or gradually, may have great potential to damage the group morale. This may result in frustrating everybody else's effort to achieve the objectives that were initiated together. Counsel has already been put in place for us in these last days to "hold fast the confession of *our* hope without wavering, He who promised is faithful" (Heb. 10:23). In addition, "not forsaking the assembling of ourselves together, as *is* the manner of some, but exhorting *one another,* and so much the more as you see the Day approaching" (Heb. 10:25).

The only valid reason to discontinue any group project is if someone discovers a conflict between that project and the Word of God. In such a case, leaders may help by engaging in wise conflict resolution and management. Sometimes there is little or nothing that can be done to dissuade people who have made up their minds to disconnect themselves from the church, but we must try to help them. Some will reason and argue their way out. Others may not want to share with anybody their reasons for dropping out. They simply request for their names to be deleted from the Church books. People who drop out of their Church and renounce their spirituality hurt those with whom they previously fellowshipped. Worse still are those in leadership who completely give up their faith. As we near the end of time, we should not be surprised that there will be dropouts, just as there were just before Israel crossed the Jordan.

In the last book of the Bible, the Greek verb *nikáw—*"to conquer," "overcome," "vanquish," "subdue," "be victorious," "prevail"—appears seventeen times in its different forms (Rev. 2:7, 11, 17, 26; Rev. 3:5, 12, 21; Rev. 5:5; Rev. 6:2; Rev. 11:7; Rev. 12:11; Rev. 13:7; Rev. 15:2; Rev. 17:14; Rev. 21:7). The word also implies "to come off superior in a judicial cause" (Rev. 5:5).[84] When *nikáw* is used of believers in the time of the end, it depicts the idea that whoever intentionally overcomes the trials from the enemy of God will receive heavenly inheritance. Prevailing over evil is apparent for the believer. Jesus Christ, who loves us, enables us to pass the test; see Romans 8:37.

Problem Solving

When people differ in opinion, it often creates hostility, and hostility usually ends up in separation. Shortly before the time for Moses to lay down the mantle of leadership, he was approached by this group of representatives from two and a half tribes. These men had a petition,

---

[84] Wesley J. Perschbacher, ed., *The New Analytical Greek Lexicon* (Peabody, MA: Hendrickson Publishers, 2001), 284.

and they articulated their case very clearly. They pointed out to Moses that the land east of the Jordan was vacant. They specified, "the country which the LORD defeated before the congregation of Israel, is a land for livestock, and your servants have livestock" (Num. 32:4). When Moses heard the request of the leaders, he at first gave them a negative response (Num. 32:6–15). He immediately assumed that they were trying to get out of doing the hard work required to subdue the land of Canaan. But the leaders of the tribes of Reuben and Gad were not easily offended, and neither were they easily deterred. They realized that Moses's concern was real. In fact, it almost seems that they had expected it, and they were prepared with a reasonable response. Instead of being disheartened, they "drew near" to Moses. You can almost hear them lowering their voices in deference to his authority, yet with the confidence of their case (Num. 32:16–19). Perhaps they had prayed over this matter and received wisdom from the Lord before ever they came to Moses. It may well be that some in this delegation had been with Moses and heard the Lord's message regarding this land on the eastern side of the Jordan. God had said, "'Rise, take your journey, and cross over the River Arnon. Look, I have given into your hand Sihon the Amorite, king of Heshbon, and his land. Begin to possess *it,* and engage him in battle'" (Deut. 2:24). "And the LORD said to me, 'See, I have begun to give Sihon and his land over to you. Begin to possess *it,* that you may inherit his land'" (Deut. 2:31; see also Deut. 3:2, 18). Moses seems to have forgotten about this instruction.

Armed with the confidence that their request was in harmony with God's counsel, yet with a humility that assured Moses of their good intentions, the petitioners suggested a solution to the concerns of the aged leader that erased any fears that their goal was to separate from their brethren, or to leave the difficult work to others. They bound themselves with an oath to go with their brethren and work to clear the land of Canaan from any impediments that might prevent the other nine and a half tribes from settling in their new homesteads. Moses saw that his fears were unfounded; his concerns were alleviated. It seems that Moses, in granting the petition of the leaders of the tribes of Reuben and Gad and half of the tribe of Manasseh, was actually acting on the counsel of God.

The idea of beginning to grant the inheritance by settling some of the tribes of Israel was God's in the first place. It was not an arbitrary decision on the part of Moses. The fact that Moses rendered his final verdict in the presence of, and with at least tacit support from, Eleazar the priest gives credence to the understanding that the Lord must have been guiding a prayerful Moses in his answer to the men of Reuben and Gad. He was given the wisdom to balance the different aspects of his answer with great diplomacy. He did give permission for Reuben and Gad and half of Manasseh to settle in their desired location, but this was dependent upon their willingness to take up the oath of service for which they had volunteered.

The men of the two-and-a-half tribes must bind their constituents with a pledge to go over Jordan and fight alongside their fellow tribes for the liberation of the land of Canaan. Not until the task of subduing Canaan was deemed complete by the leader of Israel would these men be at liberty to come back to the east side of the river and settle down with their families and their herds. By this wise arrangement, schism in the camp of the Israelites was avoided. No other tribe could feel that they were discriminated against. The "family" of Israel was bonded together in cooperation toward a common set of goals, even though a mighty river would flow between their territories. This last bit of diplomacy on the part of Moses clearly demonstrates that he had learned not to make choices based upon his own wisdom, but rather that he sought God for guidance in everything.

The summary of the petition brought by the elders to Moses was succinct and clear: "Do not take us over the Jordan" (Num. 32:5). Moses well knew that it was very dangerous for a leader to strive for political correctness rather than divine principle. God must never be left out of any part of our existence, even if we think that we know the right thing to do. A leader is always safe when one makes decisions backed up by God's word. Problems are best solved in light of God's counsel; this glorifies God. We are now living under very uncertain circumstances where reliance on God is necessary even with regard to seemingly simple and straightforward decisions. Often our first answer will be changed by God's wisdom. Whatever it is, take it to the Lord in prayer!

End of Journey

It is important to keep in mind the goal we want to achieve. If it be a race, we want to finish the race. We want to finish strong. If it be schooling, we want to get the qualification. If we embark on a journey, we want to get to our destination. Someone said that it took God one night to pull Israel out of Egypt, but it took forty years to get Egypt out of Israel. They took forty years instead of the expected two weeks to get to their destination. It was their stubbornness, rudeness, covetousness, greediness, and ungratefulness that extended Israel's journey to forty years. Many people failed to arrive at the Jordan because they decided to cling to rebellion and died in the wilderness. Despite the unfaithfulness and incessant grumbling of the multitudes of Israel, we see God loving, forgiving, providing, delivering, disciplining, and saving. Thank God for being who He is! His mercy endures forever!

Once the mind is set on accomplishing something, experience has taught us that there are bound to be obstacles along the way. Obstacles can be positively utilized to assess our progress, sharpen our focus, plan new strategies, and utilize our resources well. The journey must be completed. For those of us who are aiming for heaven, we must press on until we get there. Jesus wants everybody there! What we should be aware of is that there is a possibility that some people may not get to heaven. Jesus cautioned, "Enter by the narrow gate; for wide *is* the gate and broad *is* the way that leads to destruction, and there are many who go in by it. Because narrow *is* the gate and difficult *is* the way which leads to life, and there are few who find it" (Matt. 7:13–14). All provisions are in place for all people to be in heaven. Yet like those who fell away along the journey to Canaan, some people may be obstructed by what they encounter on the way. They are fascinated by temporal worldly things and so lose their goal of eternal life.

It should be noted here that wealth is often a hindrance to our success in reaching the Promised Land. Some people get rich while others do not, even when they're sometimes given the same opportunities. Riches that are obtained through devious means do not glorify God. We should remember that it is God who makes us rich. Everything belongs to God. We are just stewards entrusted with that which belongs to God. We are accountable to God for everything He hands to us. When we have an increase in our resources, we should not forget that it is God who grants blessings to us.

When God outlined the borders of the land of Canaan pertaining to the nine and one-half tribes which were to cross over Jordan, He reiterated to Moses in Numbers 34:1–15 that Reuben and Gad and the half-tribe of Manasseh were already situated and did not need to be included in the division of the land for the other tribes on the western side of the river. Interestingly, God restated that the boundaries designated in this chapter excluded the land that was already given to the two and a half tribes according to God's counsel in Deuteronomy 2:31, stating that Reuben, Gad, and the half-tribe of Manasseh had already received their inheritance (Num. 34:13–14). In fact, God instructed that the eastern border of the land given to the other nine and one-half tribes would run from the eastern side of the Sea of Chinnereth (Sea of Galilee), and "shall go down along the Jordan, and it shall end at the Salt Sea" (Num. 34:12), now known as the Dead Sea. Because the river might be a problem to a fugitive from the law, God told Moses to locate some cities of refuge on the east side of the river so that the murderer could flee there. Six of such cities were to be scattered in the nation. God specifically assigned three cities to be east of the Jordan and three west of the Jordan. We see God's grace in this provision of safety for those who were not guilty of premeditated murder, but who had accidentally killed someone. Moses again outlined that the boundaries of Israel would include the territory of Lebanon and as far as the great river, the River Euphrates (Deut. 1:7; Deut. 11:24; Josh. 1:4; 2 Sam. 8:3).

By choosing not to cross over, the two and a half tribes had already calculated that there would not be enough land for everybody on the other side. If they believed there was enough land across the Jordan, then we might suspect that it was mere greediness that prompted these folks to stay behind. We know that it took quite a long time for the nine and one-half tribes who crossed over Jordan to settle in because they could not drive out the nations. God informed Moses that the land was large enough for them and that He was not going to drive the Canaanites out all at once, lest there be an overpopulation of wild animals that would prove dangerous to the people (Exod. 23:29–30; Deut. 7:22).

The whole world has been on a spiritual journey toward heaven for a while now. All indications show that we are in the last camp and are about to cross over. We must be alert and oriented. In this end-time "camp," while we wait for Jesus to come back as He promised, we will encounter a lot of distractions. In our case, there are many who have died, and who still will die "on this side of Jordan." It is a comfort to know that those who remain faithful to the goal but who, because of death, cannot cross over to the Promised Land during their lifetimes will not be forgotten. They are included in the territory to be inherited by those who are translated (1 Thess. 4:16–17). God does not leave any of His faithful children out of His plans for the Promised Land. Those who remain alive and are preparing for heaven must be ready to cross over, and they must rid themselves of all entanglements that might prevent safe passage. Never allow distractions. Many people will lose all hope for going to heaven. The Bible does warn us of the dangers for all people in the time of the end. It does not look good for many. Yet those who remain faithful will triumphantly cross over into heaven.

Many people like to stay outside the limits of God's word. Some people no longer believe the Bible and conclude that it is too rigid. Others slide outside the Church because the Church is understood as too restrictive. Many folks have already attained what they want to live for; they have found their heaven here on earth. They have what they need and do not see any reason to think about eternity. They rationalize and justify the reasons for their lack of interest in heavenly things. Once people apostatize, it becomes harder to convince them to come back to the faith. "For *it is* impossible for those who were once enlightened, and have tasted the heavenly gift, and have become partakers of the Holy Spirit, and have tasted the good word of God and the powers of the age to come, if they fall away, to renew them again to repentance, since they crucify again for themselves the Son of God, and put *Him* to an open shame" (Heb. 6:4–6).

There is nothing so deadly for anyone as spiritual complacency (see Rev. 3:17–18). When people make a commitment to obey and serve God while they continue to live lives short of righteousness, they are heading for disaster. The Church was commissioned to go into the world and preach the gospel to all people so that they can be ready for the second coming of Jesus. The sad thing is that the world has crept so far into the Church that many of those who were aiming for heaven are disoriented. The desire to go to heaven is still there, but the life in accordance with the culture of heaven is lacking. Many in the Church betray righteousness for sin.

On our life pilgrimage, let us not settle for this earth. We are aiming for heaven. Heaven is real; do not settle for less. Beware: the world is passing away and its lust, but anyone who does the will of God abides forever (1 John 2:17).

Chapter 10

THE LAW AGAIN

WE LIKE THE law, especially when it protects us and serves our interests. We also expect other people to regard the law so that they will not hurt us or infringe upon our rights. What we do not particularly want is to be implicated by the law or be obligated to keep it ourselves. We do not want anyone or anything to make us feel guilty. Thus we tend to resist and often find ways to evade or escape the law if possible. The law can be tampered with in many ways. The guilty often go free while the innocent suffer the tyranny of injustice.

However imperfect laws may be, life on earth is not worth living without a universal law that is either respected by or enforced upon all people. The law of God is different from human laws in that every aspect of God's law is for our own good. God has given us guidelines so that we can function and behave according to His benevolent expectations.

While the people of Israel were in their last camp by the Jordan River, Moses began repeating and emphasizing the instructions God had given for them to live by if they were to be successful in Canaan. Moses's farewell speech received its title from its first two words in Hebrew, *'elleh haddebarim,* or "these are the words." In short, the speech could be titled *debarim,* meaning "the words" (Deut. 1:1). This work is known to us today as Deuteronomy, meaning "repetition of the law." The word *Deuteronomy* came from the Septuagint's (the pre-Christian Greek translation of the Old Testament) rendering of a phrase in Deuteronomy 17:18. The title Deuteronomy is also fitting because the book reiterates the law of God to help prepare Israel for their new lives under God's leadership. Just before crossing into the free land, the law became crucial because it served as the covenant between God and the people. Moses began this work by briefly recapping their travels from Mount Sinai/Horeb through the wanderings in the wilderness. The rest of the book is a reiteration, elaboration, and highlighting of God's law. He also stressed the importance of obedience once the congregation reached Canaan.

Moses called all people to pay attention as he began his detailed legal deliberations. He advised, "Now, O Israel, listen to the statutes and the judgments which I teach you to observe, that you may live, and go in and possess the land which the LORD God of your fathers is giving you" (Deut. 4:1). Moses had given some of these laws before at Mount Sinai. On the Plains of Moab, he was repeating, and possibly elaborating upon or laying emphasis on, the importance of those instructions. The people were in their last camp and hoping to be in Canaan as soon as that camp would break. Previously, at the camp at Mount Sinai, they witnessed some dramatic events when God gave them the commandments. Nothing of the sort of drama they witnessed at Sinai was evident here on the banks of Jordan. It was simply Moses reminding Israel that their future relationship with the God of their fathers was based on the guidelines that they were given earlier on. The importance of the law is seen in how it was emphasized as Israel was on the verge of crossing over into the land of promise.

The stipulations Moses reiterated were divine. They were not subject to any change or alteration (Deut. 4:2). These laws were given by God. No human being had authority to tamper with any of them. God wrote the Ten Commandments on a stone with His own finger (Exod. 24:12; Exod. 31:18; Exod. 32:15–16; Exod. 34:1; Deut. 10:2–4). To edit—or as Moses puts it, to add to or subtract from—the law of God implies sovereignty over God. Humans cannot change the law of God. They can only think or intend to change the law of God (Dan. 7:25). No portion of scripture therefore is susceptible to alteration by anyone (Rev. 22:18–19). However, humans can choose to break the law of God or to substitute their own stipulations in its place. When people break God's law, it compromises their relationship with each other and with God.

Moses pointed to a recent incident on the Plains of Moab that had claimed twenty-four thousand lives of those who disobeyed the law of

God (Deut. 4:3; Num. 25:1–9). Moses commended his surviving audience for their faithfulness thus far. In fact, he told them that they were alive up to that moment because they had chosen to abide by what God had commanded them. He reminded them that they were witnesses to God's methods of dealing with those who chose the path of disobedience. By pointing out previous punishment on those who had broken God's law and suffered for purposeful rebellion, Moses demonstrated the fact that disregarding God's law for whatever reason was consequential. Then Moses further cautioned, "Therefore be careful to observe *them;* for this *is* your wisdom and your understanding in the sight of the peoples who will hear all these statutes, and say, 'Surely this great nation *is* a wise and understanding people'" (Deut. 4:6).

At the Plains of Moab, we see Moses's four-pronged motivational strategy for Israel to regard the law of God. First, he told them to listen to the statutes and judgments outlined by God (Deut. 4:1). This would let them live. Second, Moses urged them not to add to or subtract from that which God Himself had stipulated (Deut. 4:2). Authority to modify the laws of God in any way was never given to humans. The law of God stands as it is for their welfare. Third, the people were reminded of past events which served as warnings against breaching the laws of God (Deut. 4:3). Those who broke the laws of God were subject to God's retributive judgment. Finally, observance of God's laws would grant Israel wisdom and understanding that will be acknowledged by other nations who do not worship the God of Israel (Deut. 4:6).

Balaam, hired prophet of curses and blessings, failed to inflict curses on Israel. God prohibited him from causing any harm. Trouble came to them only after they began to rebel against God's commandments. Moses explained that even after they arrived at their destination, deliberately breaking God's law would unleash the curses upon them (Deut. 27–28).

Covenantal Relationship

The Ten Commandments are meant to foster a saving relationship between God and the people who believe in His name. This can be vividly illustrated through the ancient Near Eastern covenantal contracts. When a king was defeated, he became subject to the ruler whose armies proved superior to his own. The defeated king was also required to pay allegiance and tribute as determined by his new master. In fact, the two unequal parties made a covenant treaty. The stipulations of such a covenant were drawn and administered by the more powerful king. A closer look at the stipulations of the said covenant reveals that there were rules to be observed by the subordinate nation. Some curses and blessings were included in such a covenant. The curses spelled out what the lesser power would suffer should they fail to live up to the original arrangement. The superior king would protect the defeated king as long as that king remained submissive and loyal. If the inferior power defaulted or rebelled, he would face the fury of the superior power and be severely punished. He could suffer capital punishment for breaking the covenant relationship.

Covenants between nations were meant for the protection of the minor nation. The superior power could also benefit from the material or monetary tribute paid by the weaker power. The relationship between God and His people can be viewed in light of the ancient covenantal treaties between nations. God made a covenant with His people. God gave His commandments to be the guiding principles for sustaining the saving relationship between the divine and the human. As long as the people of Israel complied with the expectations of God's law, life would be safe, fulfilling, successful, and enjoyable. Failing to keep the covenant would result in individual or national disaster. Abrogating the covenant of God by replacing any portion of it with human inventions is defying the authority of God.

It is relevant here to add greater clarity regarding God's covenant with human beings. Theological studies have defined for us what can be distinguished as the old and new covenants. We can look back to Mount Sinai, where ancient Israel camped when they came out of Egypt. God instructed them, "Now therefore, if you will indeed obey My voice and keep My covenant, then you shall be a special treasure to Me above all people; for all the earth *is* Mine" (Exod. 19:5). The Ten Commandments serve as the stipulations of the covenant between God and His people. In fact, the Ten Commandments are viewed as "the words of the covenant" (Exod. 34:28) that God established with Israel at Mount Sinai. Anyone who is willing to enter into a covenant with God will obediently subscribe to the covenant's stipulations, which are the moral law.

The Ark of the Covenant (Num. 10:33; Num. 14:44) housed the two stone tablets where the law was inscribed by God's own finger (Exod. 31:18). The people of Israel were not faithful in adhering to the requirements of God. Again and again, God sent them messengers and prophets to remind them of their obligations but to no avail. So God raised up Jeremiah the prophet, who declared the will of God.

> Behold, the days are coming, says the LORD, when I will make a new covenant with the house of Israel and with the house of Judah— not according to the covenant that I made with their fathers in the day *that* I took them by the hand to lead them out of the land of Egypt, My covenant which they broke, though I was a husband to them, says the LORD. But this *is* the covenant that I will make with the house of Israel after those days, says the LORD: I will put My law in their minds, and write it on their hearts; and I will be their God, and they shall be My people (Jer. 31:31–33; see also Jer. 32:37–41).

Other prophets expounded on the new covenant motif also (Isa. 55:3; Isa. 59:21; Ezek. 16:60; Ezek. 37:26; Hosea 2:18). Both the old and new covenants deal with the law of God. There is no covenant between God and humans without the law.

God wrote the old covenant on stone for His people at Mount Sinai. This covenant failed because the people defaulted. God, in His goodness, came up with the "new covenant" as Jeremiah puts it. With this new covenant, God would write His laws, not on tablets of stone, but in the hearts and minds of His people. The conditions of the covenant are still the same. The law is still the same too. The old covenant was made new through the provisions of the grace of God. The relationship between God and His people is still the same. He remains God and they are His people. The stipulations are still the same, the demands are still the same, the expectations are still the same, and the rewards are still the same. God's covenant, whether new or old, has salvific intent. God loves people and extends His salvation to all. God's plan is to have a saving relationship with people.

The New Testament does not establish another covenant. The same old-covenant-made-new is maintained throughout the New Testament. Zechariah welcomes the Lord God of Israel who came "To perform the mercy *promised* to our fathers and to remember His holy covenant" (Luke 1:72). Peter preached in the Jerusalem temple and reminded the people that they were the children of the covenant God made with their ancestors (Acts 3:25). Paul quotes Isaiah 27:9 on the covenant in Romans 11:27. He points out to the Galatians that the law cannot annul the covenant that was established by God in Christ (Gal. 3:17). The book of Hebrews addresses covenant issues extensively. It highlights the prominence of Jesus Christ who is "the same yesterday, today and forever" (Heb. 13:8). It is in Jesus that the covenant of God to save humanity is fulfilled in a better way (Heb. 8:6–13; Heb. 9:1–4; Heb. 10:16, 29; Heb. 12:24; Heb. 13:20; Rom. 9:4; Eph. 2:12).

Salvation and the Law

All aspects of human life and activity are directly addressed by the law of God. The moral law is best exemplified by the Ten Commandments (Exod. 20:3–17; Deut. 5:6–21). In sum, the Ten Commandments are the prescription for our conduct, faith, and worship. These ten laws are binding, immutable, and valid. In fact, God's "law is a transcript of His own character, and it is the standard of all character. This infinite standard is presented to all that there may be no mistake in regard to the kind of people whom God will have to compose His kingdom."[85]

The Ten Commandments are unchangeable and stand distinct from other laws. They cover all aspects of life including religious, legal, health, ceremonial, economic, and social life (Exod. 20:3–23:19; Lev. 1–27; Num. 15; Num. 19; Num. 28–30; Num. 35–36; Deut. 5:6–21; Deut. 12–26). The vocabulary used to describe the law is voluminous. The

---

[85] White, *Christ's Object Lessons*, 340.

Bible interchangeably uses terms such as commandments, commands, Decalogue, decrees, instructions, judgments, law, precepts, principles, regulations, rules, statutes, stipulations, teaching, and words. These different words are synonymous terms for covenant obligations. Each of these terms presents a different nuance of the law of God to enable us a more comprehensive understanding of God's covenant expectations.

No matter what we choose to call it, the law does not save anyone. Our salvation does not come from observance of the law. The law is powerless and mute when we cry out for help to overcome. Salvation is not the purpose of the law. However, the law does have its own purpose which is vitally important. We can liken the law to a speed limit sign by the roadside. We can choose to respect the sign or ignore it. We sometimes speed faster than the law allows without getting stopped by the police officer. We must not, therefore, assume that this indicates that the law which governs speeding on that section of the road has been done away with. We may choose not to obey the speed limit law, but that will eventually lead us to be under the condemnation imposed upon speeders when those who administer the law catch up with us. It is definite that on the Judgment Day, God will catch up with those who have willfully disregarded His law. Acts 17:31 announces the Judgment Day. See also Ecclesiastes 12:13–14, Matthew 12:36, Romans 2:16, 1 Corinthians 4:5, and 2 Corinthians 5:10–11.

The law then serves as a standard for judgment. There is no judgment without the law. What would be the purpose of judgment without the law? We do not keep the law to be saved, but as evidence that the grace of God was poured on us (Titus 2:11–12). It should be further noted here that grace has no definition without a law that is binding. If the law is no longer in force, then there is no such thing as grace. This thought bears contemplation. It is the goodness of God that leads us to repentance (Rom. 2:4). Obedience springs out of love for Jesus and admiration of His goodness and grace in working out our salvation (John 14:15).

Jesus and the Law of God

It is interesting to explore the way Jesus dealt with the law of God. First of all, He was a law-abiding citizen, even though some individuals were of a different opinion. We know that His enemies tried to find something legitimate for which to condemn Him, but they blatantly failed. In His famous sermon on the mountain, Jesus told the crowd that He did not come to obliterate the law (Matt. 5:17). Not a tittle will be scratched away from the law of God (Matt. 5:18; Luke 16:17). Jesus declared that His mission was to fulfill the law and the prophets (Matt. 5:17). To fulfill is to bring to completion or reality; it means to keep on record, or realize. It never means to do away with something as some minds would like to think. At one time, Jesus told a man that if he wanted eternal life, he should keep the law (Matt. 19:17–19). Jesus's teaching covered all the aspects of the law of God. There is no incident where Jesus denigrated any of the Ten Commandments as invalid or obsolete. It was the misunderstanding of, and false teachings regarding all the commandments that Jesus consistently corrected.

The religious leaders who militated against Jesus had misconceptions regarding all of the Ten Commandments, yet they read and strictly kept their interpretations of these laws. In our contemporary world, there are still gross misunderstandings of the Ten Commandments. Many Christians observe eight or nine commandments, but this is a fatal error according to James 2:10 and Proverbs 28:9. The second commandment has been completely dropped by some religious traditions because they love to worship images. The fourth commandment is blatantly rejected by the Christian majority and ascribed as belonging to the Jewish people, Seventh-day Adventists, and a few others. The example of Jesus in upholding and teaching about the Sabbath commandment is ignored by many today. There is some consolation in the fact that some people do acknowledge the biblical teaching on all the Ten Commandments. By loving and obeying Jesus, these people live in accordance to the expectations of God. Jesus affirmed all of the Ten Commandments as a vital component of our relationship with Him (John 14:15). Jesus's last call to a dying world is for us to fear God and worship Him because it is the time of His judgment (Rev. 14:6–7). The saints of God will patiently persevere in keeping God's commandments and having faith in Jesus as their Lord and Savior (Rev. 14:12).

Jesus and the Ten Commandments

1. **No other gods**: Matt. 6:24; Matt. 22:37–38; Mark 7:8–9; Mark 12:29–30; Luke 16:13
2. **No image nor its worship**: Matt. 4:10; Luke 4:8
3. **No taking the Lord's name in vain**: Matt. 6:9; Matt. 7:21–23; Luke 6:46; Luke 11:2
4. **Remember the Sabbath**: Matt. 12:1–12; Matt. 24:20; Mark 2:27–28; Mark 3:4; Luke 4:16; Luke 6:5, 9; Luke 13:15—16; Luke 14:3, 5; John 7:22—23
5. **Honor Father and Mother**: Matt. 10:37; Matt. 15:4–6; Matt. 19:19; Mark 7:10–12; Mark 10:19; Luke 18:20
6. **No murder**: Matt. 5:21; Matt. 19:18; Mark 7:21; Mark 10:19; Mark 13:12; Luke 18:20
7. **No adultery**: Matt. 5:27, 32; Matt. 19:9, 18; Mark 7:21; Mark 8:38; Mark 10:11–12, 19; Luke 16:18; Luke 18:20
8. **No stealing**: Matt. 19:18; Mark 10:19; Luke 18:20; John 10:1, 10
9. **No lying**: Matt. 12:36–37; Matt. 19:18; Mark 10:19; Luke 18:20
10. **No coveting**: Matt. 5:28–30; Matt. 22:39; Mark 12:31; Luke 10:27; Luke 12:15

Nailed to the Cross

The argument that the law was nailed to the cross, making it obsolete for us today, is blind to common sense. The context of Colossians 2:14–23 has nothing to do with the moral law of God. Specifically, the text here is not addressing the Ten Commandments as we know them from Exodus 20:3–17, Deuteronomy 5:6–21 or other biblical passages. Any food, drink, festival, new moon, or Sabbath days that were a shadow of things to come and were pointing to Christ's sacrifice on the cross are addressed in Colossians 2:14–23. All rituals for the sacrificial system were foreshadowing Christ. When Christ died on the cross, He fulfilled the demands of the sacrificial system. The laws to do with rituals were nailed to the cross because they ended in Christ. The moral laws of God, or rather, the Ten Commandments, are still binding. The cross of Christ leads us to be obedient and moral. There is no morality without the Ten Commandments. Without the Ten Commandments we become wicked and so nullify the sacrifice of Christ on the cross.

We are no longer required to follow the prescriptions of sacrificial rituals. No one should enforce the observance of these ceremonial rituals.

> Basic Sabbath rest on the seventh day of every week was not a ceremonial observance dependent on the ritual system. It preceded the ritual system and celebrated the Creation 'birthday' of Planet Earth (Gen. 2:2, 3; Ex. 16:22–30; 20:11; 31:17). However, the ritual system honored the Sabbath by the sacrifice of two additional lambs (Num. 28:9, 10) and by renewal of the 'bread of presence' ("shewbread") inside the sanctuary (Lev. 24:8).[86]

Christ, the Lamb of God, did away with the ceremonial Sabbath days. We are no longer required to do sacrifices on certain Sabbaths, as was demanded by the sacrificial system (see Numbers 28, Numbers 29, 2 Chronicles 31:3, and Colossians 2:14-23). Nevertheless, Christ never obliterated the observance of the weekly seventh day Sabbath. He went to the place of worship on Sabbath "as His custom was" (Luke 4:16). Also, "at new moons, which began the months, the priests presented a group of additional burnt offerings and one purification ("sin") offering. Along with their grain and drink accompaniments, they presumably supplemented the regular morning burnt offering (Num. 28:11–15)."[87] However, "Isaiah 66:22, 23 prophesies that all people will worship God on new moons and Sabbaths in 'the new heavens and the new earth.' Since the basic meaning of new moons and weekly Sabbaths is to celebrate God as Creator, their relevance will outlive the problem of sin."[88]

---

[86] Roy Gane, *In the Shadow of the Shekinah* (Hagerstown, MD: Review and Herald Publishing Association, 2009), 142.

[87] Ibid.

[88] Ibid., 142–143.

If the Ten Commandments were done away with at the cross, the apostles would have illustrated that. Paul demonstrated that not being under the law but under grace is no permission to sin (Rom. 6:15). He continued to write that the law has dominion over humans as long as we are alive (Rom. 7:1), that the law is not sin (Rom. 7:7), that the law is holy (Rom. 7:12), and that he delights in the law of God (Rom. 7:22). Paul also validates that he would not have known sin if there was no law (Rom. 7:7). James 2:10 points out that anyone failing in one point of the law is guilty of breaking the whole law. First John 3:4 defines sin as the transgression of the law. As long as we have the thing called sin, then the law binds.

Law in the Time of the End

Just as Moses reminded ancient Israel about the law of God when they were at the border of the Promised Land, it is very important for us who live at the end of the end-time to consider the importance of the law of God. This is doubly urgent as we prepare for the judgment that precedes the transition into eternal life. We cannot simply rationalize and discard the law of God as impotent because of Christ's atonement on the cross (Rom. 6:15). Sin is lawlessness (1 John 3:4). The Bible talks about judgment. In fact, the judgment motif runs through both Old and New Testaments. God is introduced as Judge of all the earth (Gen. 18:25; Deut. 32:36; 1 Sam. 2:10; Heb. 10:30). The righteous and unrighteous both receive judgment from God according to their works (Eccl. 3:17; Eccl. 12:14; Acts 17:31). There is ample evidence in the Bible that there is coming a judgment from which nobody will be able to escape. Judgment will occur because the law of God still stands.

The last days on earth are chaotic. The whole earth is in constant trauma, not only from natural catastrophes but more so from disasters caused by humans. Accidents (on land, underground, in the air, and in the sea), diseases, earthquakes, murder, starvation, suicide bombings, terrorism, slavery, and war, ravage our world today and claim millions of lives. On the other hand, abuse, crime, divorce, drug addiction, rebellion, robbery, and gun violence send shockwaves of horror through our communities today. People live in fear. Many are fainting due to fear (Luke 21:25–26). The once-secure nations now panic daily because of imminent terrorism and uncertainty.

Lawlessness abounds everywhere. In some places, law enforcement is utterly unable to cope with the situation. Sometimes when law enforcement officers respond to emergency calls, they become vulnerable to gun violence. People are in desperation. *Terror* is an active word in the news rooms. Human distress worsens with the coming of the lawless one prior to the end of the world (2 Thess. 2:7–12). Our days are evil and are worsening each moment. Violence statistics are soaring high and alarming. Desperation is felt everywhere; there is no safe place. We are in a crisis. It seems everything is getting out of control despite the effort to bring back sanity and the rule of law. It is time for us to realize that we are heading toward the very end of everything.

The Bible is not silent about the abuse of God's law at the time of the end. God calls all people to pay attention to His law. An attempt to change God's times and laws characterizes the last days (Dan. 7:25). The end-of-time struggle between the dragon, Satan (Rev. 12:9; Rev. 20:2), and the woman, the Church (Rev. 12:17), is focused on the children of the woman (believers) because they keep the commandments of God. Satan rages against those who are obedient to God, and he attempts to destroy them. Revelation 14:12 speaks of the patience of "those who keep the commandments of God and the faith of Jesus." The evidence of our commitment to Jesus as our Lord and Savior is revealed by keeping the commandments of God. Jesus said, "If you love Me, keep My commandments" (John 14:15). Just before the Bible ends, the declaration is made: "Blessed are those who do His commandments, that they may have the right to the tree of life, and may enter through the gates into the city" (Rev. 22:14). Those who are truly committed to God will keep His Ten Commandments to the very end. They do this not to be saved, but as evidence that they have been transformed by the grace of God (see Titus 2:11–14).

Chapter 11

DEATH OF A NATIONAL HERO

NO HUMAN LEADER has ever attained to the level of authentic leadership that Moses reached during the forty years he spent leading Israel out of Egypt to the Land of Promise. Moses wrote of himself that he was "very humble, more than any man who was on the face of the earth" (Num. 12:3). To speak of oneself like this could easily be perceived as being pompous; such statements are only considered proper when other people speak well of one's virtues. Someone else eulogizes us; it is not our place to speak in favor of our own character and reputation. However, the Hebrew adjective *'ānāw* of Moses means "poor, lowly, bowed down, insignificant, humble,"[89] "needy, afflicted,"[90] and "oppressed."[91] Also, "it never means 'meek.'"[92] In addition, "*'ānāw* means, basically, bent over (under the pressure of circumstances) and consequently, as affliction does its proper work, humble."[93] This word "expresses the intended outcome of affliction: humility."[94]

The context of Numbers 12:3 illuminates our understanding of the supposed humility of Moses. It began with Miriam, the big sister, supported by Aaron, the big brother. The older siblings spoke against

---

[89] *TLOT*, 2:934.

[90] *NIDOTTE*, 3:454.

[91] *The Complete Word Study Dictionary: Old Testament*, eds. Warren Baker and Eugene Carpenter (Chattanooga, TN: AMG Publishers, 2003), 852.

[92] Jacob Milgrom, *The JPS Torah Commentary: Numbers* (Philadelphia: Jewish Publication Society, 1990), 94.

[93] *NIDOTTE*, 3:455.

[94] *TWOT*, 2:682.

their younger brother Moses on two counts (Num. 12:1–2). Miriam and Aaron were Hebrew supremacists who disgruntled over Moses's dark-skinned wife. Subsequently, they also challenged Moses's authority, saying that he was not the only spokesperson able to speak for God. Moses, the national leader, is being discredited here by his own siblings. Moses already had many of the Israelites contending against him. Now his own family is seeking to humiliate him. Soon most of the Hebrew community would stand behind Miriam and Aaron in attacking Moses. The future was starting to look really bad. But God intervened immediately (Num. 12:4). It is always wonderful to experience divine intervention. Many times God seems remote and uninvolved. The silence, or seeming absence, of God when we need Him has bothered many believers. God does care. He is involved in all our affairs even though we do not always see immediate evidence of the fact. It is true that God does amazing things to protect and provide for us.

Moses was badly hurt by Miriam and Aaron. As the context demonstrates, 'ānāw "stresses the moral and spiritual condition of the godly as the goal of affliction implying that this state is joined with a suffering life rather than with one of worldly happiness and abundance."[95] When we have the ability to pay evil back and we choose not to, rather leaving vengeance as God's prerogative and not our own, then we will be walking in Moses's footsteps. This attack on Moses was personal, yet he did not choose to fight back. He allowed the full course of this affliction to develop and produce the intended nasty outcome—that is, to reduce him to nothingness before all of the people. The attack against Moses by Miriam and Aaron was two-pronged. His family and his calling from God were the only assets Moses had for himself. His siblings threatened to dismantle his family and discredit his connection with God. If this had been allowed to happen, Moses would have been stripped of everything he was and everything for which he stood. Moses chose to suffer this devastating humiliation from his siblings rather than defending himself from their atrocious attack. God honored the humility and patience of His suffering servant, and dealt with the perpetrators Himself.

---

[95] Ibid.

No human being has ever had an experience with God like the experience of Moses. When Moses was under this unreasonable attack from his own siblings, God immediately came down from heaven to defend Moses. God is a defender of the defenseless (see Ps. 59:1–2). God informed Aaron and Miriam of Moses's faithfulness among all people. Of Moses, God declared, "I speak with him face to face, even plainly, and not in dark sayings; and he sees the form of the LORD. Why then were you not afraid to speak against My servant Moses?" (Num. 12:8). God was angry against Miriam and Aaron. Miriam became a leper instantly; Aaron, the only one of his siblings who never had leprosy, turned out to be a passionate confessor and intercessor! Moses was vindicated, and God demonstrated to all of the people that speaking against the servant of the Lord is taboo.

Why Miriam alone was punished by God is a puzzle. It may be that she was the one who instigated the whole hurtful incident. Accusing her brother for marrying Zipporah was a racial slur. Racism still drives many people crazy today, even believers. Attacking Moses for assuming too much by taking it upon himself to be the only spokesperson for God was untrue and irresponsible. Moses had pleaded with God that the burden of leading the people was too heavy for him (Num. 11:14). God asked Moses to bring seventy elders from Israel to share the leadership burden and all these seventy men prophesied (Num. 11:24–25). Moses wished all people to be prophets of God (Num. 11:29). Miriam's accusations were unreasonable. Sin is always unreasonable and cannot be excused. The Lord's solution for sin is one of two things: either repentance and pardon, or punishment.

Instructions Are Necessary

Moses was faithful to God to the very end. Of course, the seasoned leader was human, and he made many mistakes during his career. One such incident stands out near the end of Moses's life. The people complained bitterly for water. They had done this many times before. This time it was in Kadesh, and the congregation was particularly bitter against both Moses and Aaron. It was bad. The Lord arrived at the scene and talked to Moses. "Take the rod; you and your brother Aaron gather the congregation together. Speak to the rock before their eyes, and it will yield its water; thus you shall bring water for them out of the rock, and give drink to the congregation and their animals" (Num. 20:8). Thank God for His intervening grace!

A good worker always does what is expected of him. Moses promptly responded to God's directive. Along with Aaron, he brought all of the people before the designated rock. Then it was that Moses made the greatest mistake of his life. He lifted up his voice and chided the people. "Hear now, you rebels! Must we bring water for you out of this rock?" (Num. 20:10). While everyone watched intently, Moses lifted up that famous rod of the Lord and struck the rock again (Num. 20:11) as he had done in the past (Exod. 17:6). Water gushed out, and the excited crowd turned its attention from Moses to the water. But the Lord was not so easily distracted. He came to Moses and told him that he had not followed instructions (Num. 20:12). The leader had been instructed to lift up his voice and talk to the rock, but Moses lifted up his voice and cursed the audience! He did not speak to the rock at all. If God takes the trouble to say something, He expects His people to pay close attention to what He says. There is no way to accomplish God's will except for simple obedience to His bidding. It sometimes seems possible to accomplish what we want through devious means; we may even see a blessing in that. But no grain of disobedience will ever win God's approval. Apparent success in ministry, if accomplished through some deviation from God's outlined principles, is no guarantee of God's acceptance.

The Lord is good. Water gushed out of the rock, and the thirsty crowd was hydrated. Despite Moses's failure to follow instructions, God gave water to the people. Oftentimes we do wrong things in an attempt to advance God's kingdom. God may grant us success, but it does not mean that He overlooks our deliberate or well-meaning mistakes. We are accountable to God for our words and our actions. God may bless His work despite our weaknesses, but He does not ignore our carelessness in following His instructions. The task may be accomplished, but if we have failed to follow God's directions for the accomplishing His will, we still stand condemned. Our success in God's work does not override our accountability to Him. God does not respect anyone who chooses not to cooperate with, and carefully follow His divine will. Those who serve the Lord will learn sooner or later that carelessness, selfishness, stubbornness, and wickedness, this quartet of self-will, does not go unchecked for long. We must not be content with accomplishing our ideas of God's will by any means outside His clear direction. Strict obedience is vital in maintaining a saving relationship with Him. God is righteous, and He accepts our efforts only when they are based upon actually obeying Him.

Just after Moses hit the rock for the second time in disobedience to God's clear command, he was informed of the penalty. What he did was going to cost him the one thing he had worked for these past many years. His leadership contract with God would be terminated before Israel would cross over into the land of Canaan (Num. 20:12). There are no words to describe the depth of the heartache that Moses must have felt upon hearing these words. His repentance was immediate and deep, but God could not excuse the transgression lightly. It is a credit to the great meekness of the tried and tempted and deeply disappointed leader that he continued to lead Israel in honoring God after he knew that he would not be allowed to cross into the Land of Promise with the people. Moses faithfully executed his duties to the very time God called him away to his death. The one burden of Moses's remaining days was to see Israel successful in following God when they finally arrived in Canaan without him.

Close to Home

Israel journeyed until they came to the final camp on the Plains of Moab by the Jordan River across from Jericho (Num. 33:48–50). This camp was the last one before Israel crossed over into Canaan. This was as far as Moses's leadership would go. Many people have experienced this kind of leadership scenario; they lead for years through thick and thin, only to be relieved of their responsibilities at the verge of a great breakthrough. The incoming leader takes over and easily crosses over, appearing to achieve the long-anticipated goals. This successor gets the credit, but in reality it was the groundwork accomplished by the deposed leader that made the success possible. In the case of Moses, the Lord allowed a special favor. The old man would not lead the people over the Jordan, but Moses was allowed to go and view the land from the top of Mount Abarim/Nebo/Pisgah before he died (Num. 27:12–13). The reason for his failure to successfully lead Israel into Canaan was spelled out clearly to him. He had rebelled against the command of the Lord to hallow Him at the rock as the people watched (Num. 27:14).

It is important to understand something of the reason for the harsh sentence against Moses after his unfortunate words and actions at the second striking of the rock. What Moses did at Kadesh was not simply hitting a rock for a second time. He rebelled against a plain command of the Lord. Sin is always rebellion against God's commands. As in the case of Moses, we usually do not know how grievously our rebellion may affect the onlookers. Moses destroyed an important object lesson, thus preventing many from gaining a deeper understanding of the ways and plans of God for Israel's salvation.

God has good reason to treat rebellion seriously. Another example is that of King Saul, the first king of Israel. He failed to follow the instructions of the Lord. He spared that which he was supposed to destroy. King Saul had a "good" intent; he believed he followed God's instructions and in addition had spared some animals for sacrifices. The prophet-priest Samuel brought Saul's mistake before him in its true light.

> Has the Lord *as great* delight in burnt offerings and sacrifices, as in obeying the voice of the Lord? Behold, to obey is better than sacrifice, and to heed than the fat of rams. For rebellion *is as* the sin of witchcraft, and stubbornness *is as* iniquity and idolatry. Because you have rejected the word of the Lord, He also has rejected you from *being* king (1 Sam. 15:22–23).

Sin has been defined as "transgression of the law" (1 John 3:4 KJV). When we simply fail to follow any of God's commands, it is sin. God will hold us accountable. It is wonderful to sincerely do God's will exactly as He intends for it to be done. If God gives us specifics, He also enables us to accomplish the same. God's grace is sufficient for all that we need while we are on His mission. Compromise and shortcuts never glorify Him. Simple and unquestioning obedience to God is expected of every believer.

While Moses continued his work of preparing the people for their transition into the Promised Land, he received a word from God. "Take vengeance on the Midianites for the children of Israel. Afterward you shall be gathered to your people" (Num. 31:2). The Lord does not forget. Moses had to carry on his last assignment with the knowledge that he was going to die soon after it was accomplished.

For many people, death comes unexpectedly. We all die; the important thing is the kind of death we will experience. God's truth shines out always: Moses accepted God's truth about himself, and although he was punished, he repented honestly, returned to his habit of obeying God implicitly, and died at peace with God and man. "Precious in the sight of the LORD is the death of His saints" (Ps. 116:15). This is the only kind of death I recommend for you, for myself, and for everybody. There is hope in the death of the righteous because God shall surely raise us from the dead (Isa. 26:19; Dan. 12:2; John 5:28–29; 1 Thess. 4:16; 1 Cor. 15:52; Rev. 20:6).

Blame Game

Again and again, Moses reminded Israel that he could not go into Canaan because of them. Moses felt that his wrong actions were Israel's fault. He opined, "The LORD was also angry with me for your sakes, saying, 'Even you shall not go in there'" (Deut. 1:37). Although it was true that the people had provoked Moses viciously, Moses was still responsible for his own actions. Israel could not have forced Moses to hit the rock for the second time. They didn't even suggest it; it was his own action. His own mismanagement of his personal anger ruined his privilege of completing the journey into Canaan. Moses should not have hit the rock. He should have spoken to it according to the word of the Lord.

When we go wrong, we often want to point to others as being responsible for our mistakes. This blame game started in Genesis 3.

Adam blamed Eve and God. Eve blamed the snake. Of course, the devil who spoke through the snake blamed God. We humans should know by now that blaming others for our own faults will not help us resolve a problem in any way. Blaming others only complicates our relationships with those individuals. God is honored when we acknowledge our sins and accept the consequences of our behavior. God has a way for each one of us to be rescued from the results of our mistakes if we will, as Moses did, repent and accept God's discipline. It is much better to avoid blaming each other for our faults. "If we confess our sins, He is faithful and just to forgive us *our* sins and to cleanse us from all unrighteousness" (1 John 1:9). We should be thankful for this mercy. In addition, we are encouraged to confess our sins one to another and pray for each other (James 5:16).

Moses must have prayed seriously for God to give a second opinion regarding His punishment for that fatal sin at the rock. Moses told Israel that God was angry with him and that God would not listen to his pleading for permission to go into Canaan in spite of his sin (Deut. 3:26; Deut. 4:21; Deut. 34:4). God even told Moses to quit asking about going into Canaan. This is not the only time we see God rejecting an individual's plea for God to rescind a consequence of transgression. David pleaded for the life of the child he had begotten with another man's wife, but God did not change His mind; the child died (2 Sam. 12:13–20). Paul prayed repeatedly for relief from a health condition that was debilitating (2 Cor. 12:7–10). What Paul was suffering from might have been consequential. The Lord did not give Paul the pain relief for which he begged.

The restlessness and murmuring of the Children of Israel may have goaded Moses to the point of speaking and acting unadvisedly. However, Moses alone was responsible for his actions, and he accepted that responsibility. In telling them that they were the cause of his inability to go over before them into Canaan, Moses was pointing out the fact that their bad behavior was the trigger for his disobedient actions. We would do well to accept this as an object lesson. Our negative behavior may have adverse effects upon others. Jesus took this concept of responsibility for someone else's sin to another level. He said that causing other people to sin is a fatal error. "Whoever causes one of these little ones who believe in Me to sin, it would be better for him if a millstone were hung around his neck, and he were drowned in the depth of the sea. Woe to the world because of offenses! For offenses must come, but woe to that man by whom the offense comes!" (Matt. 18:6–7). Avoid tempting anyone into disobeying God.

Moses experienced the reality that God is gracious, but He does not compromise. Moses warned the tribes that were preparing to cross into Canaan that they must always keep God's commandments. If they ever, at any time in their existence, failed to do so, their sin would find them out (Num. 32:23). When we go through a devastating experience and learn from our own mistakes, it is always important to warn other people so that they will not repeat our foolish mistakes. The old saying that experience is the best teacher makes sense. Moses, the leader, had warned other people to be careful in their relationship with God. Now he is experiencing the results of his own failure. He had seen many people perish because of disobedience, but now it was his turn. The message is clear. Because Moses blundered, he reaped the consequences of his wrong. Now he encouraged others to be careful to obey God.

We are held accountable for our own disobedience. I admire individuals who, having contracted a sexually transmitted, life-threatening disease, admit their plight and disseminate a warning message to help others beware of following in their disobedient ways. I also appreciate those who publicly reveal their deviant sexual orientation. Such people, if they are willing, can receive tremendous spiritual support and assistance that may lead them to recovery. We should be good students who learn from the mistakes of others, and we should allow others to learn from our own mistakes.

Beginning Right and Ending Wrong

Although Moses himself had a burning desire to get into the Promised Land, God refused him entrance because he had rebelled against God on the way from Egypt. From this incident, we discover that someone may begin well, but by committing sin, he or she may forfeit the anticipated promise of salvation. Many people cherish the idea "once saved, always saved." Proponents of this thought believe that once you accept Christ wholeheartedly, you get saved and sealed for salvation for good. In other words, Jesus saves you, and you are guaranteed eternal life. It sounds good and appealing. However, several texts are used to support this idea. These include the sayings of Jesus in John 3:16, John 5:24, and John 10:27–29, which portray the concept that those who believe get everlasting life and shall never perish because no one is able to snatch them away from Him.

The Bible unequivocally states that once we are sealed in Christ, nothing shall be able to separate us from Him. Some of the texts that support this idea include Romans 8:35–39, 1 Corinthians 1:1:4–8, Ephesians 1:13–14, and Philippians 1:6. Unfortunately, all these texts and a lot more are brutally taken out of context to express the notion that when someone is saved, he or she is always saved. Believers need to understand how the Bible uses the words like *eternal* or *forever*. A good example is Jude 7. Sodom and Gomorrah were destroyed by eternal fire, but there is no fire still burning there today. The fire on those cities was eternal in the sense that it burned until there was nothing else to burn. When we believe, Jesus accepts us and grants us His eternal salvation. We receive this salvation by faith. As long as we remain faithful to Him, the promise of our salvation stands. But if we abscond the faith, live wickedly, and refuse to repent, we will be lost. Many who left Egypt wanted to get to Canaan, but they died in the way because of their sins.

God created both angels and human beings perfect. They were not programmed as mere robots but were given free will and the power of choice. God did not create Satan. He created Lucifer, who was a perfect angel. But Lucifer chose to become Satan. God never forced Lucifer against his will. We can begin well, and if we choose to part ways with God, He will not force us to continue with Him. Salvation is not by coercion. Salvation is not a trap that catches you and never lets you go. Salvation is God's promised love gift, and we receive it provisionally now by faith. Someone can receive salvation and dispose of it at own will, especially by committing sin. From the Old Testament to the New Testament, there is a clear motif that when a righteous person decides to sin, he or she will forfeit the salvation that had been received from God (Ezek. 18:24–26; 2 Pet. 2:20). Jesus expressed this concept well in the parable in Luke 12:42–48. The faithful servant who changed his mind and later did wrong things would get in trouble at the end. Saul was chosen by God to be the first king of Israel. He started well. He was filled with the Holy Spirit, and he even prophesied (1 Sam. 10:6–9; 1 Sam. 19:21–24). However, Saul made some bad choices and did not repent. God rejected King Saul for his unfaithfulness and stubbornness. Saul died hopeless.

Paul cautioned the Corinthian believers that he could preach to others, but if he failed himself to run the race of faith, he would be disqualified (1 Cor. 9:24–27). Some believers started well but gave up their faith (Gal. 1:6–10; Gal. 3:1–4). Paul pleaded with them to reconsider the truth. The saved person can backslide by choice. When he or she does so, it may be hard for that individual to surrender back to Christ as Lord and Savior (Heb. 6:4–6; Heb. 10:23–26). The end result of such a person is to be lost despite the fact that one had received God's salvation before. God's grace teaches us to shun evil (Titus 2:11–14). We cannot evade obeying the law of God because of grace (Rom. 6:14–15). It is clear that the wages of sin is death (Rom. 6:23). We are saved by faith and not by our own works. Evidence that we are saved is shown in our love for Christ and obedience to God's law (John 14:15; John 15:10; Rev. 14:12).

If we are saved in Christ, but we happen to commit sin, we need to confess our sin and make things right with God (1 John 1:9). Also, 1 John 2:1–2 advises believers that it is imperative to confess sin. If a believer does not confess, his or her own unconfessed sin will lead to destruction. We are saved now by faith when we accept Jesus as our personal savior. We have to keep the faith until our deliverance at the last time (1 Pet. 1:4–5; Heb. 11:39–40). The Bible does not contradict itself. It is very consistent in its teaching, but the problem is with those who read into the Bible their own ideas (2 Tim. 4:3–4; 2 Pet. 3:14–17). Therefore, the idea that "once saved, always saved" is not biblical at all. It is not only untrue, but a product of irresponsible hermeneutics. It gives a false hope to many people who believe that they were saved and will make it into heaven on that premise regardless of whatever or however they choose to live. We should be serious of our salvation (Matt. 7:13–14; Phil. 2:12–13).

Death at the Border

At the camp on the Plains of Moab, Moses had a great catalogue of business to take care of. He was to prepare Israel for their transition into a land that had been promised to their progenitors. Moses encouraged Israel to remain faithful to God all of the time in order to enjoy the blessing of God on their lives in Canaan. Forgetting the statues of God would cause disaster for the entire nation. God made sure that Moses reminded Israel about the consequences of wrong behavior. Moses accomplished this God-given task and made it easier for Joshua, his successor, to carry on with the mission.

People received their final instructions from Moses just before they crossed over. Many who had anticipated crossing over into Canaan failed to do so because of unruly behavior. Attracted by the culture of local women, about twenty-four thousand men were struck by a terrible death right there on the Plains of Moab, in sight of the Jordan River (Num. 25:9). These people were at the border and were about to cross over. They did not make it into the Promised Land because of their poor choices. Just think about it! Some of these people who died here may have seen the miracles of God that brought them freedom from Egyptian bondage. These people had survived and persevered through a forty-year struggle in the desert. They reached the border and then failed to enter into rest. Was it unfair of God to thus punish the disobedient ones so near to the Promised Land? I believe it was not. This was not an issue of fairness, but rather one of disobedience to God and the ultimate consequences of that disobedience.

When we choose to disobey God and sin against Him, our sin will find us out (Gen. 4:7; Num. 32:23; Isa. 59:12; Gal. 6:7). Sin defiles and corrupts. Sin is a deadly mistake. Sin transgresses God's law. Sin defaces the image of God in our souls. Sin destroys. The verdict is clear: "For the wages of sin is death, but the gift of God is eternal life in Christ Jesus our Lord" (Rom. 6:23).

It does not matter how long we have maintained our faith in the Lord; if we choose to sin, we lose everything. Our major contributions to God's Church down through the years are nullified the moment we default into sin, even at the end of our lives. We throw away the hope of getting into heaven when Jesus comes. Sin can make you a loser at the beginning, or at the end of life. Sin makes you lose all that you stood for throughout your life.

> God shut Moses out of Canaan to teach a lesson which should never be forgotten—that He requires exact obedience, and that men are to beware of taking to themselves the glory which is due to their Maker. He could not grant the prayer of Moses that he might share the inheritance of Israel, but He did not forget or forsake His repentant servant. The God of heaven understood the suffering that Moses had endured; He had noted every act of faithful service through those long years of conflict and trial. On the top of Pisgah, God called Moses to an inheritance infinitely more glorious than the earthly Canaan.[96]

Farewell

Moses charged all Israel to remain faithful to God. He called Joshua, and before the entire congregation, he gave him a final word of counsel. He gave him a charge too in the presence of all the people thus: "Be strong and of good courage, do not fear nor be afraid of them; for the LORD your God, He *is* the One who goes with you. He will not leave you nor forsake you" (Deut. 31:7). Moses then delivered the law to the priests and commanded them to be industrious and faithful religious leaders. As custodians of the law of God, the priests were to carefully instruct the nation about the requirements of God. Then Moses took Joshua to the tabernacle of meeting. The Lord appeared there in a pillar of cloud and informed Moses that it was time for him to die (Deut. 31:16). The last task Moses received from the Lord was to write a song that Israel would sing in Canaan. Moses wrote the song and taught Israel how to sing it (Deut. 31:22). The song of Moses (Deut. 32:1–43) is a long,

---

[96] Ellen G. White, *Patriarchs and Prophets* (Washington, DC: Review and Herald Publishing Association, 1890), 479.

inspiring poem. What an amazing way of ending one's ministry! When Jesus was facing betrayal and subsequent death, He sang a song with His disciples (Matt. 26:30). Moses's final act as leader of God's people was teaching them to sing a new song! It is too bad that we have lost the music to this beautiful composition, but the lesson remains: heroes of faith end their lives while singing songs of triumph! They sing songs of praises! On their death beds, the righteous of God will continue inspiring hope to those who remain. They pass on the baton of faith!

The lyrics of the song of Moses depict God as sovereign and fully involved in the life of His often-wayward people. When Moses finished teaching the people the song, he started talking to them. Moses blessed all the people (Deut. 33). Surely Moses was experiencing strong emotions as he gave his blessing and mentioned Reuben, Judah, Levi, Benjamin, Joseph, Ephraim, Manasseh, Zebulun, Issachar, Gad, Dan, Naphtali, and Asher. There is no chronological order in his recitation of these names. The veteran leader forgot Simeon, the second born of Jacob and Leah. Moses's last speech should not be compared to Jacob's last speech in Genesis 49. Moses's speech lacked the content of Jacob's insightful blessing to his progeny. However, Moses gave a long and eloquent farewell message, ending on a high note. He raised up his voice and declared,

> *There is* no one like the God of Jeshurun, w*ho* rides the heavens to help you, and in His excellency on the clouds. The eternal God *is your* refuge, and underneath *are* the everlasting arms; He will thrust out the enemy from before you, and will say, 'Destroy!' Then Israel shall dwell in safety, the fountain of Jacob alone, in a land of grain and new wine; His heavens shall also drop dew. Happy *are* you, O Israel! Who *is* like you, a people saved by the LORD, the shield of your help and the sword of your majesty! Your enemies shall submit to you, and you shall tread down their high places (Deut. 33:26–29).

Of interest here is the reference to Jeshurun, "upright one."[97] This word comes from the Hebrew root *yshr*, "be level," "straight," "(up) right," "just," "lawful,"[98] or "smooth."[99] Jeshurun is mentioned only four times in the scripture (Deut. 32:15; Deut. 33:5, 26; Isa. 44:2). The substantive Jeshurun appears in parallel with or in the context of Jacob and Israel (Deut. 33:4–5; Isa. 44:2). Therefore, Jeshurun is said to be the "honorific"[100] or "poetic name for Israel, designating it under its ideal character."[101] Moses articulated that God is the God of Jeshurun (Deut. 33:26). We understand that Israel was the custodian of God's law and stipulations. Israel was expected to be up right with God. However, Israel could only be upright by choice and through the enabling of God.

After the congregation had heard the final admonitions and received the last blessing from the leader that had interceded for them these forty years, they returned to their tents. The Lord told Moses that it was time for him to climb up Mount Nebo and die there. Without a murmur, the old patriarch started walking, all alone, to find the place where God would make his grave. Moses was still vigorous; it was not difficult for him to get up the mountain. But perhaps he climbed slowly, taking time to think back over his life. On top of Mount Nebo, the Lord showed Moses all the land that was going to be occupied by Israel. Shortly after his panoramic view of the land to which he could not go (Deut. 34:1–4), Moses died on Mount Nebo/Pisgah. Part of his eulogy reads, "Moses was one hundred and twenty years old when he died. His eyes were not dim nor his natural vigor diminished" (Deut. 34:7). Balaam the diviner once hoped out loud that his life would end like that of Moses. He sighed: "Let me die the death of the righteous, and let my end be like his!" (Num. 23:10). For Balaam, it was a passing wish. For Moses, on the other hand, righteousness was something he cherished and pursued day after day for all the years of his life. Although his faults are on record for all to read, the story of Moses is that of a faithful and triumphant friend of God.

---

[97] *BDB*, 449.
[98] *TWOT*, 1:417.
[99] *BDB*, 448.
[100] *TLOT*, 2:588.
[101] *BDB*, 449.

End-time Death and Dying

Death will continue to be a menace until Jesus comes. Many will die just before Jesus comes. The ones to die last will spend a brief moment in death. But why would they die when Jesus is about to come? We know that just before Jesus comes, there will be a terrible time of trouble such as has never been since there was a nation on earth (Dan. 12:1).

> So through this time of trouble, when those who live, will find their patience tested to the utmost, when death is upon every side, and anguish, too deep for utterance, fills every heart, some will sleep, free from the strife; and these are pronounced blessed by God and by the Spirit; because, they 'rest from their labors; and their works do follow them.' Having begun a good work, having accepted the everlasting Gospel with all the consequences that would follow, and having fought a good fight, Christ Himself completes what they have begun, and they rest until the announcement is made that He is coming.[102]

The prophet Isaiah had some insight into this. He declares, "Come, my people, enter your chambers, and shut your doors behind you; hide yourself, as it were, for a little moment, until the indignation is past" (Isa. 26:20).

The Bible is clear that the dead know nothing (Eccl. 9:5). They do not go to heaven (Eccl. 3:19–21). Jesus never commanded people to go to heaven when they die. Instead, Jesus said that He will come back again to get His beloved saints and take them with Him to heaven (John 14:1–3). Bible believers already know that Enoch (Gen. 5:24; Heb. 11:5) and Elijah (2 Kings 2:11) were taken to heaven alive. What puzzles many believers is the account of Elijah and Moses appearing from heaven on Mount Tabor to talk to Jesus (Matt. 17; Mark 9). The question often asked is this: How did Moses get to heaven? The Bible is clear in that Moses died on

---

[102] Stephen N. Haskell, *The Story of the Seer of Patmos* (Nashville, TN: Southern Publishing Association, 1905), 262.

Mount Nebo/Pisgah and was buried there (Deut. 34:5–6). There is also a piece of information we can decipher about what happened to Moses after he died alone on Mount Nebo/Pisgah. Jude 9 reports, "Yet Michael the archangel, in contending with the devil, when he disputed about the body of Moses, dared not bring against him a reviling accusation, but said, 'The Lord rebuke you!'" We understand that it was on this occasion that Moses was resurrected from the dead and taken to heaven. God will call some of His people to sleep just before the second coming of Jesus so that they may escape the horrific final moments of this planet earth (Isa. 26:20–21). They will be raised up to eternal life when Jesus comes.

Moses is the third human being mentioned in the Bible who has already gone to heaven. There are others, but we do not know just how many people have gone to heaven from this earth. At the death of Jesus, we read,

> And Jesus cried out again with a loud voice, and yielded up His spirit. Then, behold, the veil of the temple was torn in two from top to bottom; and the earth quaked, and the rocks were split, and the graves were opened; and many bodies of the saints who had fallen asleep were raised; and coming out of the graves after His resurrection, they went into the holy city and appeared to many (Matt. 27:50–53).

When Jesus was resurrected, many dead saints in the vicinity also were resurrected, and they went into the city and were seen by many people. In the ancient times, when a king went out to war and conquered, he would come back home with a group of captives as evidence of his successful mission. In the same way, Jesus came and defeated the enemy, Satan, and He also conquered death (Rev. 1:18). When Jesus ascended to heaven, He took some resurrected saints to heaven with Him as evidence that He had conquered the enemy and death. Therefore it is said of Jesus "When He ascended on high, He led captivity captive, and gave gifts to men" (Eph. 4:8; see also Ps. 68:18).

Moses's death just prior Israel's crossing over the Jordan into Canaan has eschatological significance. Many of the saints who will be alive just before Jesus comes will be called to sleep. This will be good for them, allowing them to escape the trying time of trouble. From Old Testament to the New Testament times, sleep has been used as a euphemism for death (Dan. 12:2; John 11:11; 1 Thess. 4:13–17). Ever since the death of Abel, the first human being to die, the Good News is that the dead shall be raised back to life again (John 5:28–29). It does not matter how or when we die; the one rewarding thing is to hear the voice of Jesus calling us back to life! The jubilant faith hero raised back to life will have time as it were to recite the poem: "O Death, where is your sting? O Hades, where is your victory?" (1 Cor. 15:55). We have all reasons to give thanks to God who gives us victory over death through our Lord Jesus Christ (1 Cor. 15:57).

Chapter 12

THE CROSSING OVER!

GOD HAS AN agenda. God takes the initiative and approaches Joshua, the son of Nun, who is the new leader of the nation of Israel. Joshua is told that it is time to lead the people across the Jordan River and so complete the forty-year journey. God assures Joshua of His divine support; his success is guaranteed. The promise is clear. God will be with Joshua wherever he goes! Nearly forty years ago, Joshua had prophesied, "If the LORD delights in us, then He will bring us into this land and give it to us, a land which flows with milk and honey" (Num. 14:8). God is faithful. The people have come from far. They have seen many demonstrations and manifestations of God's power and purpose to lead them home. Now it appears that Israel is blocked by the raging floodwaters of the Jordan River. But for once they remember that their story is filled with God's grace, protection, and providence. At this time, the majority of the children of Israel have decided to cross over into Canaan, whereas two and one-half tribes have received their inheritance already. Reuben, Gad, and the half-tribe of Manasseh will leave their wives and children on the eastern side of the River Jordan while their military men cross over with their brothers to fight for the liberation of the rest of their new homeland.

Joshua sends a delegation among the people to inform them that in three days, they will break camp and cross over the Jordan. In three days they will be home! The two and a half tribes who had decided to stay across were reminded of their choice, and the men of war from among them prepared to join their brethren in passing over the river, in spite of the fact that it seems impossible for them to do so. The congregation is now lodging by the banks of the river. They have to make provision for food to carry with them before crossing into Canaan. They have to prepare adequate meals to sustain them in case there are delays of some sort. They must take into account that there might be inadequate time to cook while fulfilling their mission. The people need to have some ready-made meals at hand to feed themselves.

For those who are living on the brink of eternity, it will be wise to have adequate spiritual food that may keep us going despite the uncertainty of the last days. This is a call to hide God's word in our hearts and minds so that we may be ready with the bread of life safely stored where no one can take it from us. The distress of the final days may not allow us adequate time to study the word of God. The scripture we retain today in our memories is all we will have to sustain us in the intense final moments of this earth. Matthew 25:1–13 should be a lesson to us as we prepare to cross over. The crime committed by the five virgin girls who were labeled foolish is that they did not have adequate oil prior the coming of the bridegroom. Adequate preparation must precede the anticipated event. There is need for a sufficient supply of the Holy Spirit in us now before the coming of Jesus our Savior. John 6:63 says, "the words that I speak unto you, they are spirit, and they are life." Waiting until the last minute to store these Spirit-filled words in our hearts and minds leads to disaster.

At the crossing of the Jordan, the ark of God becomes more prominent again. The ark can only move when the Levites carry it. The ark becomes the sign that the people are now to watch for. The people of Israel are instructed to move only after the ark of God has moved into the river. They have to follow the ark to the crossing point. However, people need to keep a respectful distance from the ark. Nobody is to come too close lest they become too familiar with the ark containing the Ten Commandments, written by the finger of God. No human hand is to touch that ark. Likewise, in the time of the end, our religious leaders must uphold the Law of God and teach people to follow it faithfully. Yet we are to keep our hands off from that law. No one is authorized to change it in any way. We are to follow, but not touch it. We know that we are not saved by keeping the Law of God. In other words, we do not keep the law in order to be saved. The timeless truth is that when Christ abides in us—when we have love and respect for His glorious character—we will allow Him to live out His Law (His character) in our lives. Keeping the Law of God becomes evidence of God's grace, which has extended His salvation to us. This grace teaches us to renounce evil and to live righteously in this present evil age (Titus 2:11–12). It is impossible to live righteously while ignoring God's complete and perfect law.

The Preparation

Joshua was ready to take charge. He addressed the crowd with the humble confidence that God would keep His word and take His people home to the promised land: "Sanctify yourselves, for tomorrow the LORD will do wonders among you" (Josh. 3:5). The Hebrew verb *qādash* and its Greek equivalent, *hagiazō,* basically mean to be "clean," "pure," "holy," "set apart," and also to "dedicate," or "consecrate."[103] The verb *sanctify* rarely appears in a secular sense, but is instead pointed to religious devotion and holiness. When used of persons, *sanctify* implies being consecrated or dedicated to God. The priests are holy to the Lord (Exod. 19:22; Exod. 28:36; Lev. 10:3). The saints are clean (John 15:3), pure in heart (Matt. 5:8), perfect (Matt. 5:48), righteous and godly (Titus 2:12), holy (1 Pet. 2:9), and set apart (Jer. 51:45; Rev. 18:4).

When used of things, time, or places, *sanctify* means being destined for sacred use. A good example is in Numbers 16:38 where *sanctify* is used of the censers. The censers had become holy by being presented to the Lord. In other words, the censers had the "set-apartness" "that disallows their being treated in a common way."[104] The sanctified time is clearly distinguished from ordinary time. God blessed the seventh day Sabbath, sanctified it, and rested from all His work (Gen. 2:3; Exod. 20:8–11; Rev. 14:12). Jesus is even Lord of the Sabbath (Matt. 12:8; Mark 2:28). Thus the Sabbath is a sign between God and His people (Exod. 31:13; Ezek. 20:12, 20). Any foreigner who joins oneself to worship God the Creator is to keep the Sabbath holy (Isa. 56:6). The temple is also a

---

[103] BDB, 872–873; *TWOT,* 2:786–787; Moulton, *The Analytical Greek Lexicon Revised,* 3.

[104] Mounce, *Mounce's Complete Expository Dictionary of Old and New Testament Words,* 611.

holy place (Acts 6:13; Acts 21:28). When people, things, time, or places are sanctified, they become sacred and are distinguished from the profane or common.

One effective way of being sanctified is surrendering the life wholly to God, the source of holiness, as His possession. God will declare holy the person consecrated to Him. Sanctify "denotes the process of the dedication and surrender of objects and persons to God whereby these are removed from the claim of the ordinary (Exod 13:2), just as God himself can appropriate certain things (Gen 2:3: the sabbath; Jer 1:5: the prophets) and will finally achieve the sanctification of his name through the people (Isa 29:23) or punish their refusal (Deut 32:51)."[105] Of interest here in Joshua 3:5 is the fact that Joshua tells the people to sanctify themselves. Such a reflexive approach demands that "one brings oneself into the condition of consecration or cultic purity."[106]

No methodology is outlined by which to achieve this. However, Israel had walked with God for forty years, so they knew exactly how to go about being sanctified. There was no question in their minds. Any believer who is acquainted with God should be in a position to know the call and the process by which they may be sanctified (Lev. 11:44–45; Num. 11:18; Josh. 7:13; 1 Sam. 16:5). The call is extended to us today: "Sanctify yourselves."

In Exodus 19:10–11, God instructed Moses to consecrate the people. This must be done because on the third day, God would come down on Mount Sinai in the sight of all people. Moses went ahead to set the boundary of the mountain in order to protect people and animals from trespassing upon sacred ground. People sanctified themselves by washing their clothes, abstaining from any sexual conduct, and making their hearts ready to meet their God. Of course, being sanctified is not limited to such activities alone. No specific rituals are outlined here for the people to consecrate themselves. God demanded to meet Moses and the people "under certain circumstances,"[107] and in response, the people had to place themselves "into a condition allowing them to approach God safely."[108]

---

[105] *EDNT*, 1:18.

[106] *TDOT*, 12:528.

[107] Ibid., 12:530.

[108] Ibid.

People must be in the right relationship with God in order to meet with Him. At the crossing of the Jordan River, we see that Joshua is reenacting the sanctifying process with which Israel was already acquainted. The people knew what to do to sanctify themselves. When God calls for us to sanctify ourselves, there is no room for carelessness or error. This call must be taken seriously. When God says that He is coming, we need to be ready for Him (Psalm 50:3).

The noun *sanctification* (Hebrew *qiddush*) "refers to the religious discipline or the process of spiritual growth by which a person increases in holiness; the consecration, usually by vow, of objects, persons, or specific times, which are thereby set apart and made subject to special ritual rules; or the formal acknowledgement of the character of sanctity attaching to persons or times."[109] The quality or sphere of holiness belongs to God. God demands humans to be holy because He Himself is holy (Lev. 11:44; Lev. 19:2; Lev. 20:7, 26; 1 Pet. 1:16). The demand for holiness and the definition of holiness are nonnegotiable. Therefore, "sacrilege, or the violation of what is holy, does not come under human jurisdiction but rather the judgement of God which normally means death."[110] It is God and God alone who sanctifies. Humans must be ready for that.

Making humans holy is God's prerogative. Our part is to get rid of everything that obstructs the process through faith. The call to be holy demands complete abstinence from all contaminants that may endanger our acceptability before God. It becomes clear that it is not our moral action (although our cooperation is necessary), but a divine enactment that makes us sanctified. Making us holy is the work of Jesus Christ. Human goodness is never good enough before God. In response to the call of God to sanctify ourselves, we need to confess our sins to one another and to God, consecrate ourselves to God, and cooperate with God always. When we have done our best to prepare to meet our God, God reads our motives and extends His grace to cover our inadequacies. It is absolutely possible through faith to "live soberly, righteously, and godly in the present age" (Titus 2:11).

---

[109] Herbert Bronstein, "Sanctification," in *The Oxford Dictionary of the Jewish Religion* (Oxford: Oxford University Press, 1997), 606.

[110] *TDNT*, 1:111.

God Exhibits!

The call to be sanctified came with an incentive to encourage compliance by the people of Israel (Josh. 3:5). They were to be sanctified because God was going to do wonders among them. It should not be a surprise that the prerequisite for what God would do was their own preparation for it. The wonders are not outlined in the text. People might have guessed what the Lord was going to do. The Jordan River was flooded over its banks at that time of the year. It presented a life-threatening hindrance to anyone seeking to cross over. Whatever the Lord would do, it must have to do with helping the people overcome the watery obstacle obstructing their way. If the crossing over was to happen at all, then it must be a huge miracle! Settling in an occupied country required still more of God's wonderful intervention and provision. The future is always made more exciting because of God's promise to demonstrate His glorious deliverance.

The Hebrew word in Joshua 3:5, *môpēt*—"marvel," "miracle," "omen," "portent," "sign," "wonder"—explains what God is going to do for His people. This same word parallels *'ôt*, which also means "miracle," "portent," "sign," "symbol," and "wonder."[111] There are other, less frequently used Hebrew terms with similar meaning found in the Old Testament, including *massâh*, "trial," "proving" (Deut. 4:34); *môrā'*, "awesome deed" (Deut. 26:8; Jer. 32:21); *mishpātim*, "divine judgments" (Exod. 7:4; Ps. 105:5); and *niplā'â*, "wonder" (Exod. 3:20).[112]

The Greek synonyms are *teras*, "prodigy," "portent," "signal act," "wonder," "miracle" (John 4:48; Acts 2:19, 43);[113] and *semeion*, "sign," "wonder," "remarkable event," "wonderful appearance," "extraordinary phenomenon," "miracle" (Matt. 24:24, 30; 1 Cor. 14:22; Rev. 12:1, 3; Rev. 15:1).[114] God's wonders are His doing!

The word *wonder* first appears in the Exodus story. It is the word used for the miraculous acts of God that He used to deliver Israel out of bondage. There is no attestation of *môpēt*, "wonder," in secular usage

---

[111] *TWOT*, 1:67.

[112] *TDOT*, 8:174; *NIDOTTE*, 2:880.

[113] Moulton, *The Analytical Greek Lexicon Revised*, 401.

[114] Ibid., 365.

in the West Semitic ancient languages. This "Hebrew term functions exclusively in theological contexts."[115] The wonders in the deliverance of God's people are exclusively God's deeds. These wonders had two kinds of significance in the situation of Israel in Egypt. Wonders were performed as signs of the extraordinary power of God to deliver to His covenant people. On the other hand, the same wonders were punishment to those who were objecting to the liberation of God's people.

The extraordinary wonders done by God for His people must not be underestimated. Believers must take them seriously. We must acknowledge that these mighty deeds are given by God (1 Kings 13:3), declared by God (1 Kings 13:3), performed by God (Ps. 105:27; Jer. 32:20), sent against the target by God (Ps. 135:9), are seen (Exod. 4:21; Deut. 29:3), and are to be remembered by the people (Deut. 7:18; Ps. 105:5).[116] The great acts of God evoke impromptu praise and proclamation on our part. We cannot be quiet when God acts. We behold His wonders in amazement. Either through fear and horror, or from the overwhelming awesomeness of God's power and supremacy, we respond. We extemporaneously shout, say things, or sing a song. Sometimes we can shake, faint, and freeze. The purpose of the wonder is to summon humans to glorify God and give Him due credit.

At the sea, Miriam was utterly awestruck by the mighty intervention of God. She and the sisters in Israel acclaimed, "Sing to the LORD, for He has triumphed gloriously! The horse and its rider He has thrown into the sea!" (Exod. 15:21). Those delivered from the intrigues of the beast will stand and sing the song of Moses the servant of God and the song of the Lamb: "Great and marvelous *are* Your works, Lord God Almighty! Just and true *are* Your ways, O King of the saints! Who shall not fear You, O Lord, and glorify Your name? For You alone are holy, for all nations shall come and worship before You. For Your judgments have been manifested" (Rev. 15:3–4).

The rod of Moses changes to a serpent and back to the rod again (Exod. 4:3–4). Moses uses this rod to perform more wonders in the presence of the pharaoh (Exod. 7–12). All the wonderful acts God did in

---

[115] *TDOT,* 8:174.
[116] *NIDOTTE,* 2:880.

releasing Israel are viewed as acts of His "great judgements" (Exod. 6:6; Exod. 7:4) against the Egyptians and their gods (Exod. 12:12). Through the wonders, Moses and Aaron were established as God's legitimate servants who were on a divinely assigned mission to set Israel free. The Egyptians should have recognized that God was working against them to free Israel through the wonders they witnessed. On the other hand, Israel should have been quick to acknowledge and declare the fact that none other than God could do the wonders that effected their release. God is good. He sustained Israel through the desert travel by displaying His mighty provisional power in supplying resources to meet their needs. As Israel stood at the bank of the Jordan River, they had plenty of reason to trust in God. But God was not yet done. God told them to be ready because He wanted to do more wonders for them when they were prepared to cross over into Canaan.

Epochs of God's Mighty Acts

The Bible can well be labeled the Book of God's unusual acts. It begins with God's mighty creative acts and continues to relate amazing ways God demonstrates His sovereign power on behalf of His created beings. The wonders God performs speak for Him. These signs and wonders are meant for God's self-revelation (Col. 1:16). The nature of God's signs and wonders is fascinating. We comprehend the signs and wonders performed by God to be miracles. God does something that is "out of the ordinary, to produce unexpected results"[117] in the accomplishing of His divine will. That is what we understand a miracle to be. Miracles either tend to suspend the laws of nature or to use the laws of nature in unusual or extraordinary ways. God's mighty acts bring immediate deliverance to God's children. They also prefigure or symbolize end-time redemption. The final goal for the mighty acts is restoration at the end; a new heaven and a new earth (2 Pet. 3:13; Rev. 21:1). Throughout scripture, the mighty acts of God can be viewed in different historical periods involving God's covenant people.

---

[117] Louis Berkhof, *Systematic Theology* (Grand Rapids: Eerdmans, 1996), 176.

1. *Creation to the flood.* Creation is the demonstration of God's mighty creative power (Gen. 1–2). Everything created is a miracle. Life is a miracle. The reason why we propound different theories on how things came into existence is because we have failed to understand the miraculous, creative power of God. He speaks, and things come into existence. Interestingly, secular scientists are confirming more and more that the evolution theory is broken and cannot be fixable. They are confirming what the advocates of intelligent design have been proclaiming ever since. Through all creation, God still intervenes by mighty demonstrations of His creative power to accomplish His divine purpose. The universal flood unleashed upon the whole earth is a miracle story (Gen. 6–8). The flood destroyed all the wicked people. Only eight righteous ones remained unscathed. Evidence of a world-wide flood is indisputable. The rainbow is a miracle that still tells today the story that God is faithful to His covenant throughout time (Gen. 9:13–17).

2. *Post-flood nations to Israel's Egyptian bondage.* After the flood, God miraculously gave different languages to the people so that they scattered themselves all over the earth, and nations were formed. God then built a nation from one man whom He chose from southern Iraq (Gen. 11:31). God accomplished a population explosion where descendants of this one man, Abram, would become as numerous as the dust of the earth (Gen. 13:16) and as many as the stars of the sky (Gen. 22:17; Gen. 26:4). But in order to achieve this, God worked out miracles. God used some barren women in the genealogy (Gen. 11:30; Gen. 25:21). At the command of God, the barren women had children. At another time some women who were capable of conceiving were made infertile (Gen. 20:18) and vice versa (Gen. 20:17). The descendents of Abram were at risk when they took up residence in Egypt. Despite this, God continued to work on increasing their numbers, regardless of the odds they faced (Exod. 1:8–22). The stories tell of the many mighty acts of God which He performed in keeping His promises to His covenant people.

3. *Exodus to the time of the Judges.* The deliverance of Israel from
   Egypt marks another dramatic intervention of God for His
   people. The land of Egypt was ravished by ten plagues until
   that nation released Israel and begged them to leave their
   country. The last seven plagues were targeted on Egyptians
   only (Exod. 8:20–12:30). The people of Israel were protected
   from the devastation they caused. While God was making the
   covenant with Israel at Sinai, His presence was characterized by
   thunder, lightning, earthquake, fire, smoke, a thick cloud on the
   mountain, and a loud trumpet that made everyone paralyzed
   with fear (Exod. 19:17–19). For forty years, Israel was sustained
   by God's mighty, providing hand throughout their desert travels.
   God brought them to the banks of the flooding Jordan River
   and blocked the river from flowing down until all Israel had
   crossed over. Life in Canaan began with a series of defeating the
   residents of that country, as long as Israel obeyed God's orders
   for destroying those nations. The life of the Hebrews in Canaan
   was marked by fluctuations between fidelity and infidelity.
   When people absconded their faith in God and worshipped
   other things, God allowed them to experience horrendous
   suffering inflicted upon them by their contemporary nations.
   When the people wholeheartedly turned back to God, He would
   intervene through miraculous signs and wonders to deliver the
   people. One at a time, God sent deliverers whom He equipped
   with special powers to overwhelm and defeat the enemies of
   God and bring relief to the covenant people.

4. *Monarchy to the Second Temple.* During this time, prophets
   were God's emissaries who were prominent for monitoring the
   nation's behavior with regard to the covenant relationship. The
   prophets were invested with extraordinary power and foresight
   that demonstrated that they were members of God's council.
   Some kings were righteous, while others were corrupt. The
   Jerusalem temple was the center of God's demonstrations of
   His mighty saving wonders. Despite the unifying influence
   of the temple services, the nation was split into two different
   political entities, Israel and Judah (1 Kings 12:16). In 722

BC, Israel was decimated by the Assyrians (2 Kings 17:6). Later, Judah was destroyed in 586 BC by the Babylonians (2 Kings 25; Jer. 39). While Judah was in Babylonian exile, God continued demonstrating His faithfulness to them through His unusual acts in support of those loyal to Him (Dan. 1–6). The struggle between false religions and the one true religion was made prominent as Israel was forced to interact with heathen neighbors. Life in exile gave God opportunity to reveal His wonders among His own people, as well as among people of the other nations with whom they lived and worked. God brought back from captivity only those who were interested in reestablishing Jerusalem as God's political and religious center. The return from captivity is marked with dramatic events that exhibited the glory of God's miracle-working power. The second temple and the walls of Jerusalem were built again, and many people witnessed the wonders God wrought for His covenant people in the process.

5. *The life of Jesus Christ.* Isaiah foretold the coming of the Messiah with great accuracy: "His name shall be called Wonderful, Counselor, Mighty God, Everlasting Father, Prince of Peace" (Isa. 9:6). Daniel also hinted on Jesus's life and ministry (Dan. 9:25–27). The entire life of Jesus was a demonstration of God's signs and wonders. Jesus performed miracles for the benefit of others, but never for Himself.[118] A closer look into the miracles of Jesus reveals that He rejected the temptation to work a miracle to benefit Himself (Matt. 4:1–10; Matt. 27:42), and He did not seek to prove His divinity (Matt. 4:5–7; Matt. 16:1–4; Luke 11:29). Jesus never performed miracles to punish anyone (Luke 9:51–56). He demonstrated the power of His word in doing miracles to bless those around Him (Mark 1:31, 41–42; Matt. 9:29). At times He told those He healed not to broadcast their story (Mark 5:43; Mark 7:36; Luke 8:56). The forgiveness of sin accompanied healing (Matt. 9:5–6; Luke 5:20; Luke 7:48). Unbelief blocked Jesus's miracles (Matt. 13:58; Mark 6:5–6). Jesus

---

[118] *NIDNTT*, 2:630–631.

laid down His life and took it up again (John 10:17–18) to defeat sin and death (Rev. 1:18). Jesus's miracles pointed to the coming universal redemption of God. In fact, Jesus demonstrated "what is the exceeding greatness of His power toward us who believe, according to the working of His mighty power" (Eph. 1:19).

6. *Christian Church to the end times.* Jesus energized the Christian Church as He commissioned His people to preach the good news of the kingdom to the ends of the earth. Their preaching, like that of their Savior, was accompanied by many miracles (Mark 16:17–18). The apostles performed mighty miracles that confirmed the power of Jesus. Preaching is to be accomplished through the "mighty signs and wonders, by the power of the Spirit of God" (Rom. 15:19). Miraculous manifestations, however, are not the test of a true disciple of Christ. The Bible gives the caution that false prophets and the devil will also perform signs and wonders in order to deceive. Both the Old Testament and the New Testament speak of false prophets and false Christs who are able to perform miracles; they also claim to be demonstrating the power of God. We have been warned to try every spirit (1 John 4:1). On this, Jesus says, "by their fruit you shall know them" (Matt. 7:15–20; Matt. 24:24). The antichrist, or the lawless one, will deceive many through powerful signs and lying wonders in his attempt to ruin those who are sincerely committed to Christ (2 Thess. 2:3–10; 1 John 2:18). Despite the gross deceptions perpetrated by the enemy in the time of the end, those who persevere in the faith of Jesus will be saved. God's people will abide by His word, take their stand for God despite persecution, and remain committed to God even at the cost of their lives. Throughout the tribulations of the last days, God displays His power to save His people through acts of deliverance and by strengthening them in His love and promises. My faith as a believer is "in the power of God" (1 Cor. 2:5). The time of the end climaxes in a very short and hectic period of time known as the time of trouble; this is the final drama the earth will witness. It is a short time preceding the second coming of Jesus. The last seven of the plagues administered

by God targeted the Egyptians only (Exod. 8:20–12:30). Those seven plagues preceded the deliverance of the people of Israel from bondage. Similarly, the seven plagues of Revelation 16 target only the wicked people who are alive just prior to the second coming of Jesus. The righteous people living at that end time will not be affected by the seven last plagues. God will miraculously deliver the righteous from these plagues just as He protected ancient Israel from the seven last plagues in Egypt. This epoch of time on earth is characterized by amazing signs of judgments on the disobedient. The righteous will experience supernatural deliverance from the devastating plagues and from the threats and persecutions of their enemies.

7. *Second coming of Jesus to the new heaven and new earth.* Soon after the plagues that target the wicked people only, Jesus will come to claim His faithful ones (John 14:1–3). God's wonder working power will call the righteous dead back to life (Dan. 12:2; John 5:28–29; 1 Thess. 4:16; 1 Cor. 15:52). The living righteous will be transformed in an instant to join the resurrected saints and meet the Lord in the air (1 Thess. 5:17). For a thousand years, the saints will be with Jesus in heaven (Rev. 20:6). A lot takes place there. After this thousand-year honeymoon (Rev. 20:7), Jesus and the saints in the "New Jerusalem City" will come down from heaven and settle on earth (Rev. 21:10). All the wicked people will be raised up, and judgment takes place. Satan features deceiving the wicked people for the last time. They will attempt to attack the city where the saints are. Fire immediately comes down from heaven and devours all the wicked people and the devil himself. This is the destruction of sin and death forever (Rev. 20:11–15). Then God, through His creative power, will make a new heaven and new earth where the righteous shall live forever (Isa. 65:17; Rev. 21:1–5).

Throughout the history of Israel, the unusual acts of God demonstrated His unflinching faithfulness to His covenant promises. When His people turned away from Him, God would let them suffer the consequences, sometimes under domination by other nations. When the people repented and turned back to God, He would restore them through supernatural interventions that demonstrated His power and might. Each of these periods of time, when God delivered and restored His people, points forward to the grand finale of all deliverances—from the tyranny of sin and death. That final deliverance is just now on its way.

Tomorrow

At the appropriate time, Joshua sent the timely message to all of the people who were camped on the banks of the river Jordan: "Sanctify yourselves, for tomorrow the LORD will do wonders among you" (Josh. 3:5). God is gracious. Whenever there is an imminent blessing or impending doom, God warns His people to be ready (Rev. 22:6). In our own day, God has already sent the last message for us to prepare because the end of all things is at hand (Rev. 14:6–12). This message resonates with the appeal of Joshua at the bank of the Jordan River. The call is for us to get rid of the moral filth that contaminates and spoils our spirituality. It is a call to set boundaries for ourselves and separate from sin in order to be dedicated to the Lord. We must not hesitate to heed the message of Revelation 14:6–12. This message is universal, and is a warning. This message is good news, and it is appealing. This message is timely and definite. This message is urgent and final. Our response to this message must be prompt and whole-hearted. God demands it. He is about to do amazing and glorious things for us. Our part is to prepare our hearts for what is coming.

God has always been faithful to His plan of saving humans from the plight of evil. He is involved in the life of His last day Church, just as He has been involved with His struggling, believing ones throughout the history of the world.

> In reviewing our past history, having traveled over every
> step of advance to our present standing, I can say, Praise
> God! As I see what God has wrought, I am filled with
> astonishment and with confidence in Christ as Leader.
> We have nothing to fear for the future, except as we shall
> forget the way the Lord has led us, and His teaching

in our past history. We are now a strong people, if we will put our trust in the Lord; for we are handling the mighty truths of the word of God. We have everything to be thankful for.[119]

The name Joshua, meaning "the Lord saves/delivers," is the Old Testament equivalent of the New Testament name Jesus. At the appropriate time, Joshua proclaimed a message to all people to sanctify themselves, for God was about to do wonders among them. This preparation was crucial and had to be done prior God's final intervention in bringing them through to their destination. Joshua successfully led Israel in crossing over into Canaan. He was the prototype of Jesus, who will appear at the end of time and deliver His people from this world to heaven. This long-anticipated Jesus has already sent the message for His people to get ready for His coming (Rev. 14:6–12).

It takes the wonders of God to deliver humans from sin and death. Time is now far advanced. We are on the threshold of eternity and have no time to waste. The call is clear, sharp, and urgent. We need to be ready to cross over into eternity. The necessary preparation for the coming of Jesus must take place now. The coming of Jesus ends the world. We know that "Christ is waiting with longing desire for the manifestation of Himself in His church. When the character of Christ shall be perfectly reproduced in His people, then He will come to claim them as His own."[120]

There is a spiritual preparation that must take place among all people before Jesus comes. In the words of Joshua, I appeal to everyone to sanctify ourselves, for tomorrow God will do wonderful things for us! Imagine! *"Eye has not seen, nor ear heard, nor have entered into the heart of man the things which God has prepared for those who love Him"* (1 Cor. 2:9).

Every Wednesday morning, I always want to drag out our trash can from the house before the garbage truck comes, so that our trash can be picked up. If our trash is not out by the roadside, the truck comes anyway as scheduled, and it does not stop. We will be stuck with that

---

[119] E. G. White, *Testimonies to Ministers and Gospel Workers* (Mountain View, CA: Pacific Press Publishing Association, 1923), 31.
[120] White, *Christ Object Lessons*, 55.

trash. It is wise to empty ourselves of all moral trash before Jesus comes. We must be spiritually clean. Sanctify yourself today, for tomorrow God will do His wonders to deliver us from this world!

When every individual's fate is decided (Dan. 7:9–10), Jesus will announce, "Let those who do wrong continue to do wrong; let those who are vile continue to be vile; let those who do right continue to do right; and let those who are holy continue to be holy" (Rev. 22:11, TNIV). It will not be long. The waiting seven angels of Revelation 16 will begin their torments one after another, pouring out their vials on the unrighteous, on those who objected to the required preparation. The wrath of God targets the disobedient people. The righteous—those who have heeded the warning message and prepared their hearts—will be protected from the seven last plagues. And then it will not be long. Soon Jesus appears as that invincible conqueror, vested with the name "KING OF KINGS AND LORD OF LORDS" (Rev. 19:16).

The dramatic coming of Jesus to deliver His people is vividly described by Paul: "For the Lord Himself will descend from heaven with a shout, with the voice of an archangel, and with the trumpet of God. And the dead in Christ will rise first" (1 Thess. 4:16), "in a moment, in the twinkling of an eye, at the last trumpet. For the trumpet will sound, and the dead will be raised incorruptible, and we shall be changed" (1 Cor. 15:52). "Then we who are alive *and* remain shall be caught up together with them in the clouds to meet the Lord in the air. And thus we shall always be with the Lord" (1 Thess. 4:17). Praise the Lord! It shall soon happen as the Lord has promised.

While we wait during this time of the end, Satan bombards us with trials and temptations. However, the Holy Spirit equips and empowers us to navigate these challenges in the strength of Christ. Our loving God educates us daily to depend upon His grace. Jesus fills us with joy and hope as we wait for the "crossing over" into heaven. What thrills us most is that it will not be long before we see Jesus! "Our God shall surely come and He shall not keep silent" (Ps. 50:3).

BIBLIOGRAPHY

Abegg, Jr., Martin, Peter Flint, and Eugene Ulrich. *The Dead Sea Scrolls Bible*. New York: HarperCollins Publishers, 1999.

Berkhof, Louis. *Systematic Theology*. Grand Rapids: Eerdmans, 1996.

Bronstein, Herbert. "Sanctification." In *The Oxford Dictionary of the Jewish Religion*. Oxford: Oxford University Press, 1997. 606.

The Brown-Driver-Briggs Hebrew and English Lexicon. Peabody, MA: Hendrickson Publishers, 1999.

Brueggemann, Walter. *Worship in Ancient Israel: An Essential Guide*. Nashville: Abingdon, 2005.

The Complete Word Study Dictionary: Old Testament. Edited by Warren Baker and Eugene Carpenter. Chattanooga, TN: AMG Publishers, 2003.

A Concise Cyclopedia of Religious Knowledge. Edited by Elias Benjamin Sanford. Hartford, CT: S. S. Scranton, 1916.

A Concise Hebrew and Aramaic Lexicon of the Old Testament. Edited by William L. Holladay. Grand Rapids: Eerdmans, 1988.

The Context of Scripture: Canonical Compositions from the Biblical World. Three volumes. Edited by William W. Hallo and K. Lawson Younger. Leiden: Brill, 2003.

Councell, Gary R. "Stewardship—A Two Way Street." *For God and Country* 3 (2016): 8–11.

Davidson, Jo Ann. "Women Bear God's Image: Considerations from a Neglected Perspective." *Andrews University Seminary Studies* 54 (2016): 31–49.

Edwards, D. Miall. "Ordain." In *The International Standard Bible Encyclopaedia*. Edited by James Orr, et al. Grand Rapids: Eerdmans, 1960. 4: 2199–2200.

Exegetical Dictionary of the New Testament. Three volumes. Edited by Horst Balz and Gerhard Schneider. Grand Rapids: Eerdmans, 1990–1993.

Fiorenza, Elisabeth Schüssler. "Feminist Hermeneutics." *Anchor Bible Dictionary*. Edited by David Noel Freedman. New York: Doubleday, 1992. 2:783–791.

Gane, Roy. *In the Shadow of the Shekinah*. Hagerstown, MD: Review and Herald Publishing Association, 2009.

Hackett, Jo Ann. "Balaam." *The Anchor Bible Dictionary*. Edited by David Noel Freedman. New York: Doubleday, 1992. 1:569–572.

Haskell, Stephen N. *The Story of the Seer of Patmos*. Nashville: Southern Publishing Association, 1905.

Hastings, James. *A Dictionary of the Bible*. New York: Charles Scribner's Sons, 1903.

Herrmann, W. "Baal." *Dictionary of Deities and Demons in the Bible*. Leiden: Brill, 1999. 132–139.

The International Standard Bible Encyclopaedia. Five volumes. Edited by James Orr. Grand Rapids: Eerdmans, 1960.

Jenni, Ernst, and Claus Westerman. *Theological Lexicon of the Old Testament*. Three volumes. Peabody, MA: Hendrickson, 1997.

Kassian, Mary A. "You've Come a Long Way, Baby!" In *Voices of the True Woman Movement: A Call to the Counter-Revolution*. Edited by Nancy Leigh DeMoss. Chicago: Moody Publishers, 2010. 49–70.

Mattingly, Gerald L. "Amalek." *Eerdmans Dictionary of the Bible*. Edited by David Noel Freedman. Grand Rapids: Eerdmans, 2000. 48–49.

Mazani, Patrick. "The Number of Israelites at the Exodus Analyzed in the Light of Archaeology and Literary Evidence." MA Thesis, Andrews University, 1999.

McCarter Jr., P. Kyle. "The Balaam Texts from Deir 'Alla: The First Combination." *Bulletin of the American Schools of Oriental Research* 237 (1980): 49–60.

Milgrom, Jacob. *The JPS Torah Commentary: Numbers*. Philadelphia: Jewish Publication Society, 1990.

Morris, L. I. "Ordination." *The New Bible Dictionary*. Edited by J. D. Douglas. Grand Rapids: Eerdmans, 1979. 912–913.

Moulton, Harold K. *The Analytical Greek Lexicon Revised*. Grand Rapids: Zondervan, 1990.

Mounce, William D. *Mounce's Complete Expository Dictionary of Old and New Testament Words.* Grand Rapids: Zondervan, 2006.

Mulder, M. J. *"ba'al." Theological Dictionary of the Old Testament.* Edited by G. Johannes Botterweck and Helmer Ringgren. Grand Rapids: Eerdmans, 1977. 2:181–200.

Musvosvi, Joel Nobel. *Vengeance in the Apocalypse.* Berrien Springs, MI: Andrews University Press, 1993.

The New International Dictionary of the Bible. Edited by J. D. Douglas and Merrill C. Tenney. Grand Rapids: Zondervan, 1987.

The New International Dictionary of New Testament Theology. Three volumes. Edited by Colin Brown. Grand Rapids: Zondervan, 1981.

New International Dictionary of Old Testament Theology and Exegesis. Five volumes. Edited by Willem A. VanGemeren. Grand Rapids: Zondervan, 1997.

Ninow, Friedbert. "Shittim." *Eerdmans Dictionary of the Bible.* Edited by David Noel Freedman. Grand Rapids: Eerdmans, 2000.

Perschbacher, Wesley J. Ed. *The New Analytical Greek Lexicon.* Peabody, MA: Hendrickson Publishers, 2001.

Peterson, D. G. "Worship." *New Dictionary of Biblical Theology.* Downers Grove, IL: InterVarsity Press, 2000. 855–863.

Phelps, Mar Anthony. "Baal." *Eerdmans Dictionary of the Bible.* Edited by David Noel Freedman. Grand Rapids: Eerdmans, 2000. 134–135.

Rainey, A. F. "Sacrifice and Offerings." *The Zondervan Pictorial Encyclopedia of the Bible.* Edited by Merril C. Tenney. Grand Rapids: Zondervan, 1976. 5:194–211.

Rendall, Frederic. "The Epistle to the Galatians." In *The Expositor's Greek Testament.* Edited by W. Robertson Nicoll. Grand Rapids: Eerdmans, 1951. 3:184.

Slayton, Joel C. "Shittim." *The Anchor Bible Dictionary.* Edited by David Noel Freedman. New York: Doubleday, 1992. 5:1222–1223.

Spico, Ceslas. *Theological Lexicon of the New Testament.* Three volumes. Peabody, MA: Hendrickson, 1996.

Stefanovic, Ranko. *Revelation of Jesus Christ: Commentary on the Book of Revelation*. Berrien Springs, MI: Andrews University Press, 2002.

Theological Dictionary of the New Testament. Ten volumes. Edited by Gerhard Kittel. Grand Rapids: Eerdmans, 2006.

Theological Dictionary of the Old Testament. Fifteen volumes. Edited by G. Johannes Botterweck and Helmer Ringgren. Grand Rapids: Eerdmans, 1974-2006.

Theological Wordbook of the Old Testament. Two volumes. Edited by R. Laird Harris, Gleason L. Archer, Jr., and Bruce K. Waltke. Chicago: Moody Press, 1980.

VanderKam, James, and Peter Flint. *The Meaning of the Dead Sea Scrolls*. New York: HarperCollins Publishers, 2002.

Walton, John H., Victor H. Matthews, and Mark W. Chavalas. *The IVP Bible Background Commentary: Old Testament*. Downers Grove, IL: IVP Academic, 2000.

Warkentin, Marjorie. *Ordination: A Biblical-Historical View*. Grand Rapids: Eerdmans, 1982.

White, Bernard. "Adam to Joshua: Tracing a Paragenealogy." *Andrews University Seminary Studies* 54 (2016): 3–29.

White, Ellen G. *Adventist Home*. Hagerstown, MD: Review and Herald Publishing Association, 1952.

_____. *Christian Service*. Hagerstown, MD: Review and Herald Publishing Association, 1925.

_____. *Christ's Object Lessons*. Berrien Springs, MI: Andrews University Press, 2015.

_____. *Early Writings*. Washington, DC: Review and Herald Publishing Association, 1945.

_____. *Education*. Mountain View, CA: Pacific Press Publishing Association, 1903.

_____. *Gospel Workers*. Washington, DC: Review and Herald Publishing Association, 1915.

_____. *Patriarchs and Prophets*. Washington, DC: Review and Herald Publishing Association, 1890.

_____. *Testimonies for the Church*. Nine volumes. Mountain View, CA: Pacific Press Publishing Association, 1948.

_____. *Testimonies to Ministers and Gospel Workers.* Mountain View, CA: Pacific Press Publishing Association, 1923.

White, W. "Ordain." *The Zondervan Pictorial Encyclopedia of the Bible.* Edited by Merrill C. Tenney. Grand Rapids: Zondervan, 1976. 4:542–543.

Wilson, Ted N. C. "An Urgent Prophetic Calling." Accessed November 14, 2013. http://www.adventistreview.org/an-urgent-prophetic-calling.

Wilson, William. *Old Testament Word Studies.* Grand Rapids: Kregel, 1978.

For In-depth Bible Studies …

www.amazingfacts.org
www.itiswritten.com
www.voiceofprophecy.com